Student Discipline,
Special Education Discipline,
Anti-Bullying
and Other Relevant Student Issues

A Guide for Practitioners

Dora Dome, Esq.

Copyright

Copyright © 2016 by Dora Dome Law

All rights reserved. When forms or sample documents are included, their use is authorized only by educators, school districts, school sites, and noncommercial entities who have purchased the book. Except for that usage, no part of this book may be reproduced or utilized in any form or by any means, electronic or mechanical, including photocopying, recording, or by any information storage and retrieval system, without permission in writing from the author.

The information contained in this book is general guidance on the implications of the laws covered and best practice protocols in implementing those laws. The information is not legal advice and should not take the place of seeking legal advice from legal counsel on specific issues. Any forms provided in this book are provided as sample guidance and should be reviewed to ensure that they are consistent with district policy and subsequent legal amendments.

Book Cover Design by Carlos R. Gomez, GomezCreativeLabs.com
Layout Design by Taisha Rucker, Esq.
Reviewed by Emily Doskow, Esq.

ISBN-13: 978-1530963546
ISBN-10: 1530963540

Contents

Foreward: Using the Law to Promote Equity and Social Justice in Public Education vi
    Rebecca Cheung
Dedication viii
About the Author ix

Part I: Student Discipline 1

1. **Student Suspensions** 3
   - Definition - What It Is and What It Isn't…
   - Legal Standard to Suspend
   - Jurisdiction to Suspend
   - Other Means of Correction

2. **Firearms, Knives and Explosives** 8

3. **Sexual Assault and Sexual Battery** 11
   - Sexual Battery
     - Misdemeanor Sexual Battery
     - Felony Sexual Battery
   - Sexual Assault
     - Rape; "Duress;" "Menace"
     - Inducing Consent to Sexual Act by Fraud or Fear
     - Sodomy
     - Lewd or Lascivious Acts Involving Children
     - Oral Copulation
     - Penetration by Foreign Object

4. **Expulsion Recommendations** 16
   - Mandatory Expulsion Recommendations
   - Discretionary Expulsion Recommendations
   - Stipulated Expulsion Recommendations

5. **Disciplinary Investigations** 19
   - Gathering Evidence
   - Searches of Pupils and Property

6. Expulsion Hearings — 30
    Creating the Expulsion packet
    Burden of Proof
    Sworn Declaration Process - Fear Declaration
    Expulsion Hearing Procedural Requirements

7. Who Gets Notice of Education Code Violations — 35
    Mandatory Reporting to Law Enforcement
    Notification to Teachers

Part II: Special Education Discipline — 37

8. Services During Short Term Suspensions — 39

9. Manifestation Determination Procedures — 41
    Removal For More Than 10 Consecutive School Days
    Series of Removals That Constitute a Pattern
    Manifestation Determination IEP

10. Special Circumstances - 45-Day Placements — 45

11. Disciplinary Appeals — 47
    Procedures
    Authority of the Hearing Officer

12. Protections for Children Not Yet Eligible for Special Education — 49
    Is the District Deemed to Have Knowledge?
    When a Basis of Knowledge Exists
    Exceptions to There Being a Basis of Knowledge
    When There is NOT a Basis of Knowledge

Part III: Bullying and Protected Classes — 53

13. Bullying in California — The Law — 55

14. Transgender Students — 59
    Federal Law Protections
    California Law Protections
    Definitions
    Practical Considerations for Schools When Supporting Gender Nonconforming Students

Part IV: Miscellaneous Topics — 67

- 15. Responding to Subpoenas For Student Records — 69
- 16. Counseling Records and Confidentiality — 74
- 17. Home Schooling and Attendance — 77
- 18. Disruptive Parents — 79

Appendix — 81

- A. Glossary — 84
- B. Student Statement Form — 87
- C. Sworn Declaration of Witness — 89
- D. Notice of Suspension Form 2015 — 91
- E. Letter Extending Suspension — 93
- F. Letter Extending Suspension.IDEA — 95
- G. Letter Terminating Expulsion.IDEA — 97
- H. Expulsion Packet Checklist — 99
- I. Expulsion Hearing List of Exhibits — 101
- J. Stipulated Expulsion — 103
- K1. CFR 300.530 Authority of school personnel — 106
- K2. CFR 300.531 Determination of setting — 110
- K3. CFR 300.532 Appeal — 111
- K4. CFR 300.533 Placement during appeals — 113
- K5. CFR 300.534 Protections for children not determined eligible for special education — 114
- K6. CFR 300.535 Referral to and action by law enforcement and judicial authorities — 116
- K7. CFR 300.536 Change of placement because of disciplinary removals — 117
- K8. CFR 300.537 State enforcement mechanisms — 119
- L. Letter to Parent Re Subpoenaed Records — 121
- M. Civility Letter 2016 — 123
- N. Cease and Desist Letter 2016 — 125

Foreward
Using The Law to Promote Equity and Social Justice in Public Education

This book has a simple goal: equip educational leaders with important legal knowledge that will help them to create more equitable processes, procedures, and practices in their schools. School leadership requires broad skill sets and knowledge related to areas such as instruction, systems thinking, creating positive climate and culture, as well as the law. Because most administrators are former classroom teachers who have expertise in instruction and curriculum, legal issues are often unfamiliar territory that can be both daunting and overwhelming. Topics ranging from child custody to student discipline to truancy and special education abound. These issues interplay with the primary mission of each school- to educate all children to their highest potential.

As a former school principal, I personally encountered many legal issues that were not discussed during my formal preparation and training. Luckily, I had experienced mentors who taught me the ropes about topics such as restraining orders and conducting investigations and cyberbullying. As I became more fluent in the language and requirements of the law, I was able to use that knowledge to be a better leader by developing more equitable processes and procedures that more effectively upheld due process rights and fair practice.

As the Program Director of the Principal Leadership Institute (PLI) at the University of California, Berkeley, I have the honor of preparing equity minded teacher leaders who aspire to work as future school leaders. Our 500+ PLI alumni serve approximately 160,000 students in over 400 schools. When I became the Program Director, I knew I wanted to hire an instructor for the Legal and Policy course who not only understood the law, but could also help students interrogate their legal responsibilities from the lens of equity and social justice. I wanted their course to provide enough legal understanding to be able to determine the most equitable path so that they could be empowered to advocate for the most socially just solution under the law. Dora Dome has designed and taught that course for the past five years for the Principal Leadership Institute at Berkeley. She is demanding- requiring students to learn the education code and the appropriate processes and timelines. Dora is critical- asking students to interrogate the unintended consequences and appropriate leadership actions. Finally, Dora is an active contributor- she is practicing in the education field and aware of the ever changing nuances to the work.

After entering leadership positions, students reach out to me to provide feedback about their preparation. Many talk about Dora's law course and how useful it has been. While this book isn't the whole course experience, I believe that it can be an important resource for school and district leaders as well as anyone else who is interested in better understanding the intricacies and nuances of these legal issues. In essence, I believe the information in this book will help you to be a better social justice leader.

Rebecca Cheung
Berkeley, CA
2016

Dedication

This book is dedicated to all educators who believe in social justice and have committed to improving their own practice in order to ensure that the rights of students are protected. I hope this book provides clarification and guidance in these complicated areas and allows the user to feel knowledgeable and empowered.

About the Author
Dora J. Dome, Esq.

Dora J. Dome has practiced Education Law for over 19 years, primarily in the areas of student issues and special education. She graduated from University of Hawaii, Richardson School of Law (J.D.) and from University of California, Los Angeles (B.A.).

She currently provides legal representation to school districts on student issues, and has renewed her emphasis on developing and conducting professional development trainings for district staff that focus on Bullying, Equity and Legal Compliance in a proactive effort to build staff capacity to address the changing needs of their students.

Ms. Dome's work with Bullying focuses on helping school districts create the necessary infrastructure to identify and address bullying in schools and to provide staff with effective strategies to respond to various forms of bullying and harassment. Her Equity trainings examine diversity and equity issues facing school districts such as examining stereotypes that impact attitudes and behavior of staff and students, identifying the harmful effects of stereotypes within the school setting, and coaching staff to develop skills to identify, interrupt and prevent discriminatory behavior. Ms. Dome's legal compliance trainings provide up-to-date information and guidance on how to 'stay legal' in the areas of special education, student discipline and Section 504.

Admitted to the Hawaii State Bar in 1996, Ms. Dome served as a special education consultant and trainer for the Hawaii State Department of Education and Hawaii State Department of Health for five years. Ms. Dome was admitted to the California Bar in 2003. She worked with the education law firm of Dannis Woliver Kelley, (fka Miller Brown and Dannis) for eight years.

Ms. Dome also regularly presents at association conferences such as ACSA, CSBA and CASCWA. She participated on the Gay & Lesbian Athletics Foundations (aka GLAF) Keynote Panel on "Race and Racism in LGBT Athletics" and presented at the NCAA Black Coaches Association Annual Conference on "Homophobia in Sports."

Ms. Dome is a Lecturer at the University of California at Berkeley, teaching Education Law and Policy in Principal Leadership Institute (PLI) Program. She was also an Adjunct Professor at Mills College teaching in the administrative credential program for soon to be administrators.

Part I
Student Discipline

1

Student Suspensions

Definition - What it is...

California Education Code 48925(d) defines suspension as removal of a pupil from ongoing instruction for adjustment purposes.   No student may be suspended from school for more than five consecutive schooldays for any single act of misconduct. A student's suspension may be extended beyond five schooldays only pending a recommendation for expulsion. A student may not be suspended from school for more than twenty (20) cumulative days in the school year. A student may be suspended for an additional ten (10) days for reassignment or adjustment purposes. When a student transfers mid-year into a new school district, it is up to the new district whether or not to begin counting days of suspension from the number of days suspended in the previous district or to start over.

What it isn't...

"Suspension" **does not mean** any of the following:

(1) Reassignment to another education program or class at the same school where the pupil will receive continuing instruction for the length of day prescribed by the governing board for pupils of the same grade level.

A pupil who is reassigned to another class, at the same grade level, and continues to receive instruction is not suspended.

(2) Referral to a certificated employee designated by the principal to advise pupils.

A pupil who is referred to an administrator or counselor, etc., for the purpose of discussing appropriateness of the pupil's behavior, **who is allowed to return to the class from which the referral came following the discussion**, is not suspended.

(3) Removal from the class, but without reassignment to another class or program, for the remainder of the class period without sending the pupil to the principal or the principal's designee as provided in Section 48910. Removal from a particular class shall not occur more than once every five schooldays.

A pupil who is referred to a "buddy classroom" for the remainder of the class period as a timeout or other intervention, is not suspended. However, this type of removal can only occur once every five schooldays. To the extent this strategy is utilized more frequently than once every five days, it would be considered a suspension and, potentially, a violation of the pupil's civil rights.

Legal Standard to Suspend

"Burden of proof" required before suspending a student from school.

There is no specific mention of burden of proof in the Education Code or underlying legal authority. The best practice for an administrator charged with deciding whether to suspend a pupil is to be convinced by a preponderance of the available evidence that suspension is justified and appropriate after meeting with the student, presenting the evidence, and soliciting the student's version of the facts.

Some states specifically set the preponderance of the evidence standard for suspensions. This is not the case in California, but the law strongly indicates a preponderance burden is appropriate. Education Code section 48900 and the following sections define offenses that are the basis for suspension, and require the authorized administrator to make findings or "determine" that an offense has occurred justifying the suspension after, absent an emergency, meeting with the student, explaining the reasons for the proposed suspension, and asking to hear the student's version of the facts.

> "A pupil shall not be suspended from school or recommended for expulsion, unless the superintendent of the school district or the principal of the school in which the pupil is enrolled determines that the pupil has committed [*the particular offense or offenses*] *(emphasis supplied)*."

Education Code section 48900.

> "Suspension by the principal, the principal's designee, or the district superintendent of schools shall be preceded by an informal conference conducted by the principal, the principal's designee, or the district superintendent of schools between the pupil and, whenever practicable, the teacher, supervisor, or school employee who referred the pupil to the principal, the principal's designee, or the district superintendent of schools. At the conference, the pupil shall be informed of the reason for the disciplinary action and the evidence against him or her, and shall be given the opportunity to present his or her version and evidence in his or her defense."

Education Code section 48911(b).

The requirements in the Education Code satisfy federal standards for the conduct of an informal "hearing" prior to suspension. The ultimate statement of this standard is the United States Supreme Court case of *Goss v. Lopez* (1975) 419 U.S. 565. The court found that a suspension is a significant deprivation of a student's right to an education, with the potential to cause serious harm to the student's reputation and future requiring at least some procedure to afford basic due process.

> "We do not believe that school authorities must be totally free from notice and hearing requirements if their schools are to operate with acceptable efficiency. Students facing temporary suspension have interests qualifying for protection of the Due Process Clause, and due process requires, in connection with a suspension of 10 days or less, that the student be given oral or written notice of the charges against him and, if he denies them, an explanation of the evidence the authorities have and an opportunity to present his side of the story. The Clause requires at least these rudimentary precautions against unfair or mistaken findings of misconduct and arbitrary exclusion from school." *Goss v. Lopez (supra) 419 U.S. at 581.*

Although no mention is made in *Goss v. Lopez* or in the Education Code regarding what burden of proof should be applied by an administrator conducting the informal presentation of evidence and invitation for an explanation before a suspension, it is clear that the administrator is charged with making a finding or findings of fact from the available information presented. The school, through an administrator in a suspension "hearing," is seeking to determine whether or not to suspend. The generally accepted legal principle, in the absence of any other provision, is that the party seeking a result in a legal proceeding has the burden to prove the proposition by a preponderance. *Schaffer v. Weast* (2005) 546 U.S. 49, 59-62

Because the administrator must make a decision based on all of the evidence presented at the relatively informal suspension conference, which the law considers a hearing, the administrator should make the determination whether to suspend based on a **preponderance of the evidence**.

Jurisdiction to Suspend - 48900(s)

A school district has jurisdiction to discipline a student for conduct violations. The act must be related to a school activity or school attendance occurring within a school under the jurisdiction of the superintendent of the school district or principal, or occurring within any other school district. A pupil may be suspended or expelled for acts that are enumerated in this section and **related to a school activity or school attendance that occur at any time**, including, but not limited to, any of the following:
 (1) While on school grounds.
 (2) While going to or coming from school.
 (3) During the lunch period whether on or off the campus.
 (4) During, or while going to or coming from, a school-sponsored activity.

Note that the jurisdictional statement described above does NOT apply to expulsion recommendations based on Education Code Section 48915. See Expulsion Recommendations for the applicable jurisdictional statement.

Other Means of Correction

When Other Means of Correction Are Required

In an effort to reduce the overuse of exclusionary discipline for all students, and in particular students of color and other marginalized groups who experience disproportionate levels of exclusionary discipline, California Education Code § 48900.5 requires that there must be evidence documented by the school that "other means of correction" have failed to bring about proper conduct prior to suspending a student, including when the student is in supervised suspension at school.

48900.5 was amended by AB 1729 to include a non-exhaustive list of examples of "other means of correction" to provide guidance and clarification to educators about the potential tools they could utilize in their efforts to respond to and correct student misbehavior. An examination of the list makes it clear that "other means of correction" does not include progressive discipline that is punitive in nature. There are a number of school districts that have incorporated many of these strategies into their discipline matrix. Yet, there are many more that still need to identify available strategies and support school sites in the implementation of alternative means of addressing student misbehavior.

Exclusionary discipline should never be the first recourse. Teachers and administrators are encouraged to consider how the proposed disciplinary consequences are designed to change the misbehavior or help the student make better choices. If the teacher or administrator is unable to articulate how the proposed consequence will help change the student's behavior or help the student make better choices, it should be considered whether the proposed consequence is appropriate or whether something else should be done in addition to the proposed consequence. Punishment, by itself, does not improve student behavior or conduct.

When Other Means of Correction Are Not Required

48900.5 allows administrators to exercise their discretion and consider suspension upon a first offence (no requirement of other means of correction) when specific conditions are met. A student, including an individual with exceptional needs, as defined in Section 56026, may be suspended, subject to Section 1415 of Title 20 of the United States Code, for any of the reasons enumerated in Section 48900 upon a first offense, if the principal or superintendent of schools determines that the pupil violated subdivision (a), (b), (c), (d), or (e) of Section 48900 or that the pupil's presence causes a danger to others. However, just because you can suspend on a first offense for some conduct violations, does not always mean you should. Administrators should always consider whether exclusionary discipline is necessary for safety reasons or whether it will change the student's behavior. If the answer is "no," then the administrator should consider alternatives to the exclusion of the student.

2

Firearms, Knives and Explosives

Firearms

Possession of a firearm is a mandatory recommendation for expulsion. It is important to know what distinguishes a "firearm" from an "imitation firearm," possession of which does not require a mandatory recommendation for expulsion.

California Penal Code 165210 defines "firearm" as "a device, designed to be used as a weapon, from which is expelled through a barrel, a projectile by the force of an explosion or other form of combustion." Therefore, the determining characteristic is whether the weapon uses an explosion or combustion to propel the projectile. If "yes," it is a firearm, requiring a mandatory recommendation for expulsion. If "no," the weapon is an imitation firearm, which does not require a mandatory recommendation for expulsion and would require "secondary findings" to support an expulsion recommendation.

Knives

Education Code 48915(g), defines a knife as "… any dirk, dagger, or other weapon with a fixed, sharpened blade fitted primarily for stabbing, a weapon with a blade fitted primarily for stabbing, a weapon with a blade longer than 3 1/2 inches, a folding knife with a blade that locks into place, or a razor with an unguarded blade."

Be aware that California Penal Code 626.10 definition of knife includes a knife with a blade longer than 2½ inches. Therefore, law enforcement may consider a weapon a knife based on Penal Code, when the weapon, in fact, does not meet the California Education Code definition of a knife.

If a school is pursuing an expulsion recommendation based on possession or brandishing a knife, it is imperative that there is evidence that the weapon used meets the 48915(g) definition of a knife and that the administrator presenting the case is clear how the weapon meets the definition of a knife.

Example:

Student brandishes what you believe to be a knife. You pursue a mandatory recommendation for expulsion based on brandishing a knife but you have not specified what characteristics make the weapon a knife. You enter a photo of the knife into the expulsion hearing. When the characteristics of the knife are examined, it is determined that it does not meet the definition of a knife and the student cannot be expelled.

Even though the weapon is called a knife, you must examine it and determine what characteristics make it a knife, such as the length of the blade or the fact that the blade locks into place. If the weapon does not meet the definition of a knife, the student can still be expelled, however the expulsion recommendation would have to be based on possession of a dangerous object and on the fact that "due to the nature of the act," brandishing the knife at another student, the student's presence on campus is a danger to the student or others. (Ed Code 48915(a)(1)(ii))

Explosives

Under Education Code section 48915, subdivision (h), "the term 'explosive' means 'destructive device' as described in Section 921 of Title 18 of the United States Code." Under this statute, a "destructive device" means **(A)** any explosive, incendiary, or poison gas; bomb; grenade; rocket having a propellant charge of more than four ounces; missile having an explosive or incendiary charge of more than one-quarter ounce; mine, or device similar to any of the devices described in the preceding clauses." 18 U.S.C. § 921(a)(4)(A).

Common denominators to the above examples of "destructive devices" are that they are weapons that are actually capable of harm by way of explosion or flammability, with the possible exception of "poison gas." The common definition of "explode" involves bursting violently, expanding with force, and projecting outwards.

Example

A student put a "chemical mixture" in a plastic bottle, which was thrown, kicked, or rolled into a group of students at a crowded assembly. The contents exploded in some fashion, with the cap remaining on the bottle. No one was injured. There were no flames, although some reported smoke. This may have been mist. You cannot prove it was smoke. You must determine whether the object constitutes an explosive device, for purposes of determining whether a recommendation of expulsion is mandatory under California Education Code section 48915(c).

An explosive device is by definition a destructive weapon, and it appears you do not have any evidence that the "chemical mixture" in the bottle was destructive or a weapon. Therefore, with the facts given, there does not appear to be sufficient evidence to prove the bottle was an explosive device. If the District could prove that the substance in the bottle was flammable or poisonous, it would be an explosive device. If the weapon does not meet the definition of an explosive, the student can still be expelled. However, the expulsion recommendation would have to be based on possession of a dangerous object and the fact that "due to the nature of the act," throwing a devise that exploded in the middle of a crowded assembly, the student's presence on campus is a danger to the student or others. (Ed Code 48915(a)(1)(ii))

3

Sexual Assault and Sexual Battery

California Education Code Sections 48900(n) and 48915(c)(4) designate conduct that amounts to a sexual battery or sexual assault as a mandatory recommendation for expulsion. However, rather than define the terms, the California Education Code references relevant California Penal Code Sections for definitions of the conduct.

Before a student is charged with sexual battery or sexual assault, the administrator must review the relevant Penal Code sections to determine which section the conduct violates and the elements of the offense that must be proved.

Sexual Battery

There are two types of sexual battery that commonly occur on school campuses, one is a misdemeanor and one is a felony. This distinction is not relevant, as both fall under 48900(n) and are subject to a mandatory recommendation for expulsion. However, being aware of the distinction between the two types of sexual battery helps an administrator understands the evidence necessary to prove the two offenses.

<u>**Misdemeanor Sexual Battery – California Penal Code 243.4(e)(1)**</u>

When looking at the definition of any offense, it is useful to think about the definition in terms of elements that must be proved to support an expulsion order. A misdemeanor sexual battery has three elements, 1) Touching an intimate part of another person, 2) if the touching is against the will of the person touched, and 3) is for the **specific** purpose of sexual arousal, sexual gratification, or sexual abuse.

Intimate Part

An "intimate part" is defined by Penal Code to be "the sexual organ, anus, groin, or buttocks of any person, and the breast of a female." So, there must be evidence that an intimate part was touched.

Against The Will of The Person Touched

This element is self-explanatory. The victim did not consent to the touching.

Specific Purpose - Sexual arousal, Sexual gratification, or Sexual abuse

The general standard to determine intent for sexual battery crimes is to look to "[A] defendant's statement of his intent and by the circumstances surrounding the commission of the act.. . . In objectively assessing a defendant's state of mind during an encounter with a victim, the trier of fact may draw inferences from his conduct, including any words the defendant has spoken. . ."*People v. Craig* (1994) 25 Cal.App.4th 1593, 1597.

Sexual Arousal or Gratification

To prove "arousal and "gratification" in reported California cases on sexual battery, the substantial evidence must support a finding that the act was committed for the purposes of sexual pleasure.

Facts that could support a finding of sexual arousal or gratification of the perpetrator include a male with an erection, exposing himself, or masturbating or attempting sexual arousal of the victim by touching the victim's intimate places or forcing the victim to touch the perpetrator in intimate places. *People v. Dixon*, 75 Cal.App.4th. 935.

Sexual Abuse

"Sexual abuse" needs to be shown by a battery on another person's "intimate part" done either to harm or humiliate that person. Therefore, it is an "either /or" element of the offense. Sexual abuse cases satisfy this element with facts showing intent to hurt or humiliate, which appear to arise more often with school-age students.

A juvenile court conviction of a 14-year-old minor male defendant who pinched the breast of a 16-year-old female victim was upheld with findings that the assault caused her emotional distress and resulted in a significant bruise. *In re Shannon T.*, 50 Cal.Rptr.3d at 565, 567. The court found that the defendant inflicted a sexual battery under § 243.4(e) with the specific purpose of sexual abuse because he first told her, "Get off the phone. You're my ho," and when the victim responded, "Whatever," and walked away, the defendant pursued her, slapped her face, grabbed her arm, and pinched her breast. Id. at 566–67.

Similarly, the court found the minor defendant committed sexual battery when he poked the center of the victim's buttocks, penetrating about an inch. Because the defendant laughed with his companions as he touched the victim and used derogatory language, the court found the evidence demonstrated the defendant's purpose was sexual abuse. *In re A.B.*, 2011 WL 193402, at *1.

Lastly, a middle school student, who slapped his classmate-victim "with an open hand in her crotch area" was guilty of misdemeanor sexual abuse under Penal Code section 243.4(e)(1). The juvenile offender blamed his friends for telling him to do it. The record showed that the victim was "mad, embarrassed, and 'kind of scared'" and chased the defendant, who "ran away laughing." These facts led the court to conclude that the defendant "understood that his action would embarrass and humiliate" the victim. *In re Carlos C.*, 2012 WL 925029 (Cal.Ct.App.2012)

Felony Sexual Battery – California Penal Code 243.4(a)

A felony sexual battery has four elements, 1) Touching an intimate part of another person, 2) while that person is unlawfully restrained by the accused or an accomplice, and, 3) if the touching is against the will of the person touched and, 4) is for the purpose of sexual arousal, sexual gratification, or sexual abuse.

As compared to a misdemeanor sexual battery, a felony sexual battery requires that the victim be unlawfully restrained and there is no requirement to establish "specific intent," only "intent."

To prove a felony sexual battery, there must be evidence of all four elements.

Unlawfully Restrained

The person must be "unlawfully restrained" during the touching. The general rule is that a person is "unlawfully restrained when his or her liberty is being controlled by words, acts or authority *of the perpetrator* aimed at depriving the person's liberty." *People v. Pahl*, (1991) 226 Cal.App.3d 1651,1661. Effectively blocking or impeding any exit the victim could take could also be considered "unlawful restraint."

See Misdemeanor Sexual Battery (above) for a more detailed analysis of the other three elements of a felony sexual battery. Although the analysis in the sexual arousal, gratification or abuse section is specifically addressing "specific intent," which is an element of a misdemeanor sexual battery, evidence that supports a finding of "specific intent" would also support a finding of "intent" in a felony battery case.

Sexual Assault

A student who commits or attempts to commit a sexual assault is subject to a mandatory recommendation for expulsion. It is important for administrators to understand that there are six (6) different offenses that are considered sexual assaults pursuant to Education Code and they must be clear which offense is being alleged to have been violated. Below are the six offenses that are sexual assaults, however, the definitions are not complete and you MUST refer to the relevant Penal Code ("PC") sections for a comprehensive definition.

Rape; "Duress;" "Menace" – California Penal Code 261

(a) Rape is an act of sexual intercourse accomplished with a person not the spouse of the perpetrator, under any of the following circumstances: (See PC for circumstances.)

Inducing consent to sexual act by fraud or fear – California Penal Code 266c

Every person who induces any other person to engage in sexual intercourse, sexual penetration, oral copulation, or sodomy when his or her consent is procured by false or fraudulent representation or pretense that is made with the intent to create fear, and which does induce fear, and that would cause a reasonable person in like circumstances to act contrary to the person's free will, and does cause the victim to so act.

Sodomy – California Penal Code 286

(a) Sodomy is sexual conduct consisting of contact between the penis of one person and the anus of another person. Any sexual penetration, however slight, is sufficient to complete the crime of sodomy.

Lewd or lascivious acts involving children – California Penal Code 288

(a) Except as provided in subdivision (i), any person who willfully and lewdly commits any lewd or lascivious act, including any of the acts constituting other crimes provided for in Part 1, upon or with the body, or any part or member thereof, of a child who is under the age of 14 years, with the intent of arousing, appealing to, or gratifying the lust, passions, or sexual desires of that person or the child.

Oral copulation – California Penal Code 288a

(a) Oral copulation is the act of copulating the mouth of one person with the sexual organ or anus of another person.

Penetration by foreign object – California Penal Code 289

(a) (1) (A) Any person who commits an act of sexual penetration when the act is accomplished against the victim's will by means of force, violence, duress, menace, or fear of immediate and unlawful bodily injury on the victim or another person.

4

Expulsion Recommendations

The CA Education Code is structured such that it presents the basic disciplinary code of conduct first in section 48900. Section 48915 then details more severe instances of conduct listed in 48900, that if violated, create an increased health or safety hazard for a school such that an expulsion recommendation may be appropriate.

As a practical matter, a recommendation for expulsion should only be made when the law requires it, pursuant to 48915(c), or when the conduct is so severe that maintaining the student on campus safely is impractical. There are three types of expulsion recommendations: mandatory, discretionary, and stipulated.

Mandatory Expulsion Recommendations – Education Code 48915(c)

There are only five (5) offenses that require a mandatory recommendation for expulsion. When a student engages in one of the five offenses, that student must be suspended and recommended for expulsion. If the governing board finds that there is "substantial evidence" establishing that the student engaged in the conduct, the governing board must expel the student. Those five offenses include: verified possession of a firearm, brandishing a knife at another person, selling a controlled substance, sexual assault or sexual battery, and possession of an explosive. **These are the only offenses that require a recommendation for expulsion.**

Also note that the conduct listed in 48915(c) must occur **at school or at a school activity off school grounds** in order for the district to have jurisdiction to recommend an expulsion based on this section.

This is a more limited jurisdiction than what applies to 48900 violations.

Discretionary Expulsion Recommendations - Education Code 48915(a)

School administrators have discretion to suspend or expel for all conduct violations, except the five listed in 48915(c). In light of the data clearly establishing the overuse of exclusionary discipline for all students and, particularly the disproportionate impact of exclusionary discipline on students of color and other marginalized groups, it is important that administrators exercise their significant discretion and understand that just because they can suspend or expel does not mean that they should.

CA Education Code 48915(a) lists conduct violations that may lead to a recommendation for expulsion: causing serious physical injury to another person not in self-defense, possession of a knife or other dangerous object, possession of a controlled substance (with exceptions), robbery or extortion, and assault or battery on a school employee. However, if the principal or designee determines that expulsion should not be recommended under the circumstances or that an alternative means of correction would address the conduct, a recommendation for expulsion should not be made for these conduct violations.

The idea that students who engage in the above listed behaviors would not be recommended for expulsion represents a shift from the practice of strictly enforcing zero tolerance policies. This shift has been embraced and supported by the state legislature in the form of legal amendments clarifying what constitutes "other means of correction," limitations added to 48900(k) removals, and clarification of conduct that does and does not violate 48915 offenses.

Also note that the conduct listed in 48915(a) must occur **at school or at a school activity off school grounds** in order for the district to have jurisdiction to recommend an expulsion based on this section. This is a more limited jurisdiction than what applies to 48900 violations.

Stipulated Expulsion Recommendations

A stipulated expulsion is basically a process that allows a student to admit guilt and waive the right to an expulsion hearing. This is a useful process when the student is not contesting the facts of the conduct violation. The value of a stipulated expulsion is that it allows for the expulsion process to be expedited, thus allowing the student to be placed in the alternative setting sooner, thereby minimizing the academic impact of the missed instruction. It also minimizes the impact on district/school/staff resources by not having to prepare for and conduct an expulsion hearing.

There is no statutory authority for stipulated expulsions. The validity of the process was upheld in Choplin v. Conejo Valley Unified School District, 903 F.Supp. 1377 (C.D. CA 1995). The case held that a person may waive a constitutional right if it can be established by clear and convincing evidence that the waiver is voluntary, knowing and intelligent and, specifically, that parents may waive the right to a pre-expulsion hearing and consent to discipline.

If your district uses the stipulated expulsion process, it is important that the Stipulation that the parties sign clearly delineates the conduct violations the student is admitting to, including the secondary findings, and the rights that the student is waiving by signing the stipulation. The stipulation should be signed by both the student and at least one parent, and appropriate school personnel. (See appendix for sample Stipulation.)

5

Disciplinary Investigations

The purpose of a disciplinary investigation is to gather sufficient evidence to determine whether there has been a conduct violation and what would be the appropriate next steps.

Gathering Evidence

Witness Interviews

Interview the Victim

Once the administrator is informed of a possible conduct violation, the first step in the process is to **interview the victim.** You want to get as much information as possible about what happened--when, where, how, who was involved, and who may have witnessed it. Have the victim write a statement about what happened. You will also want to ask the victim whether there are supports or services that the student may need to feel safe at school while the investigation is pending.

Interview the Accused

Once the victim has been interviewed, the **accused needs to be interviewed**, informed of the allegations and given an opportunity to tell her/his side of the story. Offer the accused the opportunity to provide a written statement about the incident. If the accused refuses to provide a written statement, document that the student was offered and refused to write a statement.

Interview Identified Witnesses

If you are considering an expulsion recommendation based on the alleged conduct, it's critical to interview and obtain statements from witnesses that were identified by the victim and the accused, including any witnesses with firsthand knowledge of the incident. If a staff member was a witness, s/he should be interviewed as well and asked to provide a written statement of the incident.

School districts are encouraged to have standardized witness statement forms, that are used at all levels. The witness completing the form should indicate their name, grade, summary of the incident, date, and signature, and include a declaration under penalty of perjury and the laws of the State of California that their statement is true and correct to the best of their knowledge.

Once the written statement is completed, the administrator should review it with the witness, asking any clarifying questions, and making sure that the witness has signed and dated the document. If any witness, including the accused, writes multiple versions of a witness statement, all versions of the statement should be maintained for possible use in the expulsion hearing, regardless of whether the statements are consistent or inconsistent.

Physical Evidence

During the investigation process, the administrator should be making a list of the documentary and physical evidence needed to establish the conduct violation. What evidence is needed will be determined by the conduct violations being charged.

Was a weapon involved and has it been recovered? Is there a photo of the weapon if it is not in the possession of the school administrator? Were drugs involved and have they been recovered? Is there a photo of the drugs if they are not in the possession of the school administrator? Are there photos that should be taken of the injuries? Are there screen shots of text messages or social media posts? Was the incident captured on the school's surveillance cameras and has the video footage been preserved? Do you need to obtain medical records or a police report? Have you visited the location where conduct is alleged to have occurred and do you need photos to illustrate the physical environment?

Once the administrator has identified what documentary and physical evidence is needed in the case, the next step is to determine who is in possession of the evidence. Depending on the nature of the evidence, it could be in the possession of the police (i.e. drugs/weapons), IT department (i.e.

surveillance tapes), or parents or hospital (medical records). If the case is in fact going forward to an expulsion hearing, it would be important that the administrator begin gathering the necessary evidence early in the process to ensure that the evidence is available for the expulsion hearing.

Searches of Pupils and Property

When there is an alleged conduct violation, the administrator will have to determine whether there is a need to conduct a search for physical evidence. If so, the administrator needs to be clear what the legal standard is to support a search and the allowable scope of the search.

Legal Standard

The Fourth Amendment to the United States Constitution requires law enforcement to have "probable cause" and obtain a warrant in most cases before conducting a search of persons or property. The law, however, has evolved to recognize the realities of the public school environment with the dual needs to maintain discipline and ensure security. Therefore, the probable cause standard the police must follow does not apply to schools. Administrators need to meet the relatively lower threshold of "reasonable suspicion" before conducting a search of a pupil or a pupil's locker or belongings.

<u>Mandatory Initial Analysis:</u>

Before conducting a search, the administrator must feel comfortable that these two questions are answered in the affirmative:

1. Does the administrator have a reasonable suspicion that the student has violated a school rule or the law?
2. Can the administrator clearly state what rule or law is suspected to have been violated before the search commences and limit the search to those items that are reasonably likely to reveal evidence of the violation?

<u>How do you form a *"reasonable suspicion?"*</u>

The first point, "reasonable suspicion," does require a judgment call on the administrator's part after becoming aware of some fact or information. Acting on "hunches" or "intuition" is not enough. The information to form a reasonable suspicion needs to be based on recent and credible facts, information, or circumstances that would logically lead to the conclusion that a search of specific places could lead to evidence of a violation of school rules or the law. Information from other students in most circumstances is grounds for forming a reasonable suspicion unless the informant is notoriously unreliable, obviously lying, or the statement grossly unbelievable.

Questions to consider are the relationship between the tipster and the student suspected of violating a rule or the law, the accuracy of prior information from the tipster, and whether the tipster "heard something" ("hearsay") or was an eye witness. Prior experience with the student under suspicion can also be a factor in determining reasonable suspicion.

What violation is the search "reasonably likely" to reveal evidence of?

The second point is to be certain the scope of the search is reasonable in light of what is suspected may be found. If a student tipster tells an administrator that another student brought an automatic rifle to school, searching the other student's locker is clearly allowed. A female student's small purse in this situation would not be reasonable.

The scope and nature of the search also can include factors known to the administrator such age, sex, prior discipline history, nature of the offense relative to particular problems at school, the administrator's experience with the student, the urgency of situation (e.g., the student is said to have a bomb in his backpack), the reliability of the information leading to reasonable suspicion (a surveillance video showing the pupil carrying a weapon into the school).

Examples:

1. An assistant principal is interviewing a female student who was observed by staff during lunch period smoking in the girls' restroom. The assistant principal can smell tobacco on her breath although she denies that she smokes. These facts create a reasonable suspicion that she could have tobacco products in her purse. A complete search of her purse under these circumstances is legal even if evidence of further violations is uncovered such as marijuana, cigarette papers, and a list of what appear to be customers to whom the student is selling marijuana.

2. A student walks into class and tosses his backpack onto a metal cabinet and a loud thud follows. A

search of the backpack to see if a weapon is inside is reasonable.

3. An administrator suspects a student is under the influence of alcohol at a school function and takes the student into a private office and asks the student to blow on the administrator's face. This is a reasonable procedure.

Be certain not to impute reasonable suspicion, which may have been present in earlier instances, to be automatically applicable to later events. Each search must be based on specific and recent reasonable suspicion.

Consent Searches

Best practice is to ask the student's permission to search. It is often surprising that students will consent to searches when contraband or weapons may be readily found. Also, do not be convinced that a refusal of a request to search is an indicator of guilt. If there is an independent basis to form a reasonable suspicion, the search should proceed even with a refusal from the student.

Written consent in advance also will support a universal search of all student property in a specific group, such as bags, purses, and items brought on a field trip, particularly if there is a past issue with drugs or other contraband found on past trips even if the incidents were few and far between.

Searches of Items in Plain View

Reasonable suspicion is only needed as a precursor to a search of items not in sight. If an administrator sees something in plain view, such as a weapon on a car seat in the parking lot, or drugs dropping out of a student's pocket, immediate confiscation is appropriate. Additionally, it is not improper for an administrator to walk through the school parking lot looking into cars or looking into open lockers while patrolling hallways. If the administrator sees contraband, it may be immediately seized. Reasonable suspicion is not necessary.

Checklist for Searches:

After a reasonable suspicion to search is established by the administrator, best practices for searches include the following:

- All searches, particularly of the person, should be reasonable in scope and consistent with the reasonable suspicion that led to the search in the first place.
- Before a search, the student should be escorted directly to a private place after the student collects all belongings such as jacket, backpack, books, and hats without allowing stops along the way such as to a locker or restroom (an ideal place in some instances to get rid of contraband).
- Have an adult witness present from the beginning of the search until completed. This provides protection to the administrator from adverse claims from the student ("I had a one hundred dollar bill in my purse, and now it is gone").
- Searches should be conducted in private to the greatest extent possible, preferably with only the student, searcher, and witness in the room, to avoid embarrassment to the student.
- Have an administrator and adult witness of the same sex as the student conduct the search, particularly with searches of the person.
- Searches of the person should start with the student's removal of outer garments such as hats, sweaters, and coats and then the student emptying all pockets and laying the objects on a table or shelf.
- The law **does not allow** removal or arranging of a pupil's clothing to permit visual inspection of the pupil's underclothing, breasts, buttocks, or genitalia, or searches of body cavities (Education Code section 49050).
- Search of the person should be from the side of the student's body top to bottom, covering the forearms, thighs, and back, by crushing the fabric of the clothing rather than patting which may miss flat objects.
- Continue through all items to be searched even if contraband is found.
- Go through items set aside, including those from the pockets, thumb carefully through books and disassemble items in which contraband could conceivably be hidden.
- Locker searches should be, if possible, with the student present but not near the locker, removing items from top to bottom and emptying the locker completely before replacing any items. A staff witness should be stationed to observe both the locker and the student's face because often a student's gaze will go to where the contraband is located.
- Confiscated items should be photographed (next to a ruler in some instances such as knife blades to show size), placed in an envelope that is then sealed with a label identifying the student, the administrator, the witness, and the date, time, place, and circumstances of the

search. The school should have a designated person to be custodian of confiscated items which should be placed in a locked and secure place and kept for disciplinary proceedings or, if appropriate, delivery to law enforcement as soon as possible.

Cell Phone Searches

There is existing California case law recognizing reasonable suspicion searches of cell phones so long as the scope is limited to those items relevant to the particular suspicion. For instance, if a cell phone is confiscated for a use violation, the contents of the phone cannot be searched, as there is no reasonable suspicion to support the search. However, if a teacher reports that she suspects that a student has used a phone to cheat on a test, then there is reasonable suspicion to support a search of the phone's text messages and photos, which are locations where evidence of the cheating may reasonably be found.

However, effective January 1, 2016, through the enactment of SB178, which created Penal Code sections 1546-1546.4, a new law was enacted addressing warrant procedures when searching cell phones in connection with an arrest or traffic stop or seeking of information from electronic device service providers as part of a criminal investigation.

The implications of this new law on the legal standard applicable to searches by school administrators is unclear, as the new law refers to every state "government entity." Penal Code section 1546(i). School districts thus may be subject to the new requirements, because it is well established that school districts are direct political subdivisions of the state.

The question, of course, is what impact the new statutes have on the reasonable suspicion standard with regard to searching electronic devices as part of the disciplinary process. It could be argued that there should not be any change. SB178 focuses on warrants, wire taps, and other criminal law procedure based on a probable cause rationale. Nothing in SB 178 should erode the reasonable suspicion distinction for schools. Neither schools nor reasonable suspicion are mentioned in the act. The emphasis on probable cause and warrants in SB 178 would seem to indicate that if the Legislature wanted to change the established reasonable suspicion rule for schools, it would have expressly stated so. The public policy repeatedly stated in existing case law strongly supports maintaining school discipline especially to combat child pornography, harassment, and bullying. To assume schools are barred from reasonable suspicion searches is such a deviation from long-standing federal and state law, that it would be unreasonable to take that position--especially in the absence of any mention in SB178.

Unfortunately, no matter how compelling an argument may be made that nothing has changed, the reality is that SB 178 creates enough ambiguity about whether school districts must be treated like any other "government entity" that it is likely some attorneys will take a shot and challenge a reasonable suspicion search of a cell phone without express consent of the student.

It is therefore suggested that school districts be aware of this possible legal challenge, but continue as before with strict limits to cell phone searches within the ambit of reasonable suspicion and the use of ample documentation. There certainly are no guarantees, but the courts should uphold the schools' special status in matters of discipline.

Breathalyzers, Metal Detectors, Dogs and Other Random Searches

Schools have a broader authority to search and detain students than exists in the general community for law enforcement. So long as there is a "reasonable suspicion" that a violation of law or school rule has occurred, staff may investigate and search. *New Jersey v. T.L.O.*, 469 U.S. 325 (1985). In this context, requiring a student to expel breath into a breathalyzer would be tantamount to a "search."

There legally would be no basis for challenge of any breathalyzer request by District staff of a pupil who reasonably appears to be under the influence of alcohol or other illegal drugs. But how can a random check be legally justified without reasonable suspicion?

Suspicionless searches at school or school-sponsored events under certain circumstances have been upheld as permissible. Examples include the use of metal detectors (75 Ops.Cal.Atty.Gen. 155 (1992)) or drug sniffing dogs (*B.C. v. Plumas,* (9th Cir. 1999) 192 F.3d 1260). The legal rationale is the sound policies against weapons or drugs in the educational environment permits or even demands reasonable preventive steps.

The use of a breathalyzer without reasonable suspicion at a school-sponsored dance can be viewed in the same context. The means is a reasonable one to prevent against the obvious safety risk and potential harm. The United States Supreme Court upheld suspicionless urinalysis of railroad employees based on documented link between drugs and alcohol and train accidents (*Skinner v.*

Railway Labor Executives' Ass'n, (1989) 489 U.S. 602, 624) and of student athletes because of a prevalent use of drugs (*Vernonia School Dist. v. Acton,* (1995) 515 U.S. 646, at 652-53, 663).

The case for use of breathalyzers at school dances, beyond the obvious objectives of an alcohol-free event for the health and safety of the participants, will be strengthened if there is a documented history of problems with alcohol at past similar events. If the District has such a history, it would be valuable to make a general, non-specific reference to that in any initial announcement of the policy. Recent issues with alcohol use by students at school-events or in the community along with multiple advance notices will help to gather community support before implementing suspicionless screening.

The District should take steps **prior to beginning a policy of random breathalyzer testing at dances** including:
1. Advance notice that this screening will happen at all school-sponsored events through morning announcements, posters, community postings, and press releases.
2. Notice on tickets and all posters or other publicity relating to each dance.
3. Notice of the District policy in the next annual handbook distributed to parents and students.

Some California districts have adopted a policy of checking every student at the entrance to dances with a breathalyzer following substantial advance notice that this will occur. One out-of-state district requires each student to sign an agreement to submit to a breathalyzer test as a condition of attending the dance. (These options are mentioned for comparison purposes only.)

Whether the checking is for every student or random, a significant point is that dances are voluntary extra-curricular activities which are not mandatory. One anti-breathalyzer argument is that this screening will discourage attendance at school-sponsored dances. But in most instances, generally both parents and students endorse a breathalyzer policy.

The use of breathalyzers, however, is not without the risk of challenges from civil rights groups, and also poses operational challenges. The District should be prepared for civil rights complaints alleging Fourth Amendment infringement or violation of the Right of Privacy in Article 1 of the California State Constitution. Following the steps outlined below, however, will help districts combat such allegations.

Some Practical Considerations Before Implementing a Random Breathalyzer Program

Equipment

If breathalyzers are to be used at all, the District should purchase high-quality units and seek law enforcement guidance on acquisition, calibration, use, and maintenance. One of the reasons breathalyzers for alcohol detection have been used more widely in recent years is because these units have come down significantly in price.

There are media reports that breathalyzers have been developed which, in addition to alcohol, can also detect ingestion of marijuana, methamphetamines, and cocaine. These units are in actual use and very likely prohibitively priced. For current data and recommendation of units to purchase, the best source is still local law enforcement.

Use and care of the equipment

Most units require regular calibration. The manufacturer's recommendations should be followed and a maintenance and calibration log kept for each unit. Best practices are to keep the units under lock and key and limit access to specified staff who check out the units with a signature log. These steps will combat any argument of tampering or misuse.

To be prepared for challenges, only trained staff or School Resource Officers ("SRO") should use the units. Staff training is best provided by SROs or local law enforcement with training logs kept by the District to minimize potential arguments about the skill of those using the devices. Even law enforcement personnel using the breathalyzers or training for their use should have a record of training on the equipment available if this data is ever needed.

Who actually performs the checks is a question of District policy and culture. There are several practices:
1. Some districts prefer the authority figure of an SRO or other law enforcement personnel doing the screening.
2. Other districts choose trained staff for the assignment as an effort to be less intimidating to students.
3. Some districts use a two-person team, similar to a locker search. One or both may be an SRO or one or both trained staff.

Potential Problems with using Breathalyzers

As with any equipment, a breathalyzer is capable of false readings. Obviously, this can happen with a lack of maintenance or calibration. The literature indicates, however, that well maintained breathalyzers by and large are accurate. False positive readings reportedly can also occur if the subject has recently used mouthwash or is on a low carbohydrate diet. Staff should be ready to listen to pupil's explanation and make a judgment call whether there is a false positive. The District should consider having a procedure for handling a positive reading. Other than immediately barring the student from entrance to the dance or calling parents, one option is to administer a second reading ten minutes later before following disciplinary protocols.

A well planned program of random breathalyzer testing at District-sponsored dances can be legally sustained with ample advance notice, correctly maintained equipment, and trained screeners.

What are the Legal Risks to Administrators?

Conducting searches following reasonable suspicion and along the guidelines suggested above should shield an administrator from any claim of illegal search and seizure. In general, school administrators are charged with being familiar with the legal procedures and limitations discussed above. Good faith exercise of an administrator's duties consistent with these rules is almost always a defense to any legal claim. Legal liability can only result from clear and knowing violation of the law. Personal liability arises if the administrator knew or should have known an action violated a student's rights or if the action was committed maliciously to deprive the student of his or her rights or with reckless disregard of those rights. A prudent administrator who makes a sincere effort to follow the rules in the pursuit of maintaining the discipline and safety of the school should be able to avoid even the appearance of deliberately trying to deprive students' rights.

6

Expulsion Hearings

Administrators in most school districts are responsible to prepare for and present the expulsion case. The process has many procedural requirements that implicate legal concepts, such as due process, rules of evidence, and burden of proof. It is important that school administrators understand how to navigate the expulsion process to ensure that the law is followed and that the rights of students are protected.

Creating The Expulsion Packet

Once the investigation has been completed and it has been determined that an expulsion recommendation is appropriate, the next step for the administrator is to gather all the evidence and create the expulsion packet. Below is a list of the items that should be included in an expulsion packet.

- Notice of Suspension
- Principal's Recommendation for Expulsion
- Notice of Meeting to Consider Extension of Suspension
- Notice of Extension of Suspension
- Notice of Hearing Date and Charge Letter (notice)
- Incident reports/witness statements (redacted)
- Physical evidence (weapon, drugs, photos, etc.)
- Interventions and discipline tracker
- Teacher reports/ transcripts/attendance
- Any other relevant documents (e.g. continuance request, police report, "fear" declaration, etc.)

As the administrator assembles the expulsion packet, there are a few items to pay close attention to. First, ensure that the charges listed in the Notice of Hearing are accurate. The Notice of Hearing is the official list of Education Code violations and the district may only proceed at the expulsion hearing on the charges listed in the Notice of Hearing. If the Notice of Hearing lists multiple Code section violations, the administrator should understand the elements that must be proved for each section and be prepared to introduce evidence proving each charge.

Second, if witness statements are going to be introduced at the hearing, make sure the names of all students and minors are redacted.

Third, make sure any photos of physical evidence depict what you intend to show. For instance, if a picture of a knife is being introduced to establish that the weapon meets the definition of a knife based on the length of the blade, the photo should have a ruler next to the blade establishing that the blade is longer than 3 ½ inches. Additionally, make sure that any equipment needed for demonstrative evidence, such as audio or video equipment is available and in working condition for the expulsion hearing.

Lastly, if the case has been continued beyond the statutory timelines for any reason, the expulsion packet must include documentation supporting the continuance.

While the CA Education Code does not require that the expulsion packet be provided to the accused prior to the hearing, best practice is to provide the accused a copy of the expulsion packet as soon as it is available in order to give the student and their representative an opportunity to review the evidence to be presented and prepare a defense.

Burden of Proof

The burden of proof required to support an expulsion order is "substantial evidence." For an administrator presenting an expulsion case, this means that you must present evidence that "a reasonable mind could accept as adequate to support a conclusion" that the student engaged in the conduct charged.

Additionally, CA Education Code states that an expulsion order may not be based solely on "hearsay."

Hearsay, in a school disciplinary case, is a statement made outside of the expulsion hearing, that is offered in the hearing, by someone other than the declarant, as evidence to prove the truth of the matter asserted. For example, all written witness statements are hearsay because they are statements written outside of the expulsion hearing, that are being offered in the hearing, by someone other than the person who wrote the statement, and they are being offered for their truth regarding the information described in the statement.

Hearsay may be introduced in an expulsion hearing. However, there must also be "direct evidence" to support an expulsion order. Direct evidence is evidence offered at the hearing by someone with firsthand knowledge of the incident. Therefore, in addition to written witness statements, there must be a "warm body" testifying at the hearing from firsthand knowledge of the incident.

If the accused student admits to the charged conduct violation in a written statement, her/his admission is not hearsay and the written admission can be relied upon, as direct evidence, to support an expulsion order. The key is to make sure that the admission addresses the conduct violation directly. For instance, if the accused writes, "I did it," that has very little value in proving your case, as it is vague as to what the student is admitting to doing. If the student instead writes, "I sold weed to Tom at school on Monday," that admission could be relied upon to support the expulsion order for selling a controlled substance, even if no one physically testifies at the hearing. The written admission is direct evidence. Additionally, the administrator's testimony at the hearing that the accused admitted verbally to the same administrator that the student sold weed to Tom at school on Monday would also be direct evidence.

Sworn Declaration Process – "Fear Declaration"

Due to the CA Education Code's requirement that there be some "direct evidence" to support an expulsion recommendation, districts often encounter the situation where there is a witness to the conduct violation, the witness has written an incident statement (which is hearsay), yet the witness is unwilling to testify.

At this point, the administrator needs to determine why the witness is unwilling to testify. If it is because the witness does not want to be involved or does not want to "snitch," and the administrator needs the witness' testimony to support the expulsion recommendation, then the administrator would need to find a way to encourage the witness to participate in the process or the expulsion hearing cannot go forward.

However, if testifying at the hearing would cause an <u>unreasonable risk of psychological or physical harm</u> to the witness, the Education Code allows for the witness to testify via sworn declaration. This means that the witness' incident statement could be admitted into evidence as "direct evidence," an exception to the hearsay rule, and relied upon to support an expulsion order.

The first step is to document what the unreasonable risk of psychological or physical harm is. The documentation could be a written statement by the witness that the accused has a reputation for violence and has threatened to harm the witness in the past. The documentation could also be evidence that since the incident, the witness suffered severe anxiety which has manifested in the form of loss of appetite, insomnia, school anxiety, or lowered academic performance. This fear declaration should be separate from the witness' underlying incident statement documenting the conduct violation.

Once the unreasonable risk of psychological or physical harm has been verified and documented, the documentation of the fear declaration must be made part of the expulsion packet to be considered during the hearing. At some point during the expulsion hearing, the administrator must request that the governing board or the administrative panel (whichever body is hearing the case) consider the fear declaration and make a determination that there is an unreasonable risk of psychological or physical harm if the witness is forced to testify. The accused has the right to refute the evidence and argue that an unreasonable risk of psychological or physical harm does not exist. At the conclusion of the arguments, the hearing body must make a determination.

If the hearing body determines that there **is not** an unreasonable risk of psychological or physical harm, the witness' underlying incident statement may be admitted into evidence, but only as hearsay, and it cannot be relied on solely as a basis to support an expulsion order. However, if the hearing body determines that there **is** an unreasonable risk of psychological or physical harm, the witness' underlying witness statement may be admitted into evidence as "direct" evidence, and may be relied on as the only evidence to support an expulsion order.

The hearing body must clearly state on the record its findings and specifically identify the written incident statement it is admitting as direct evidence. It is important to note that the value of this process is dependent on the content of the underlying written incident statement, because only what is written in that statement will be admitted into evidence as direct evidence. For instance, if the underlying written incident statement says, "I saw Tom do it," the introduction of that observation does not prove the conduct violation. If, instead, the underlying written incident statement says, "I saw Tom tackle Bob from behind and begin punching him in the head," this observation goes directly to proving the conduct violation and makes it worthwhile to utilize the fear declaration process to get it admitted as direct evidence.

Expulsion Hearing Procedural Requirements

CA Education Code section 48918 lists the procedural requirements applicable to expulsion hearings. These procedural requirements must be adhered to in order to ensure that students facing expulsion receive their due process rights, as well as, allow school districts to take appropriate actions to ensure safety in schools.

While not exhaustive, below is a list of some of the relevant procedural requirements to keep in mind as the administrator prepares for the expulsion hearing.
- The expulsion hearing is to be held within 30 schooldays after the date that the principal or the superintendent determines that the student has committed any act in violation of § 48900.
- Notice of the hearing must be provided to the family at least 10 days prior to the hearing. (Ed. Code § 48918)
- The accused student has the right to be represented by counsel or a non-attorney advisor. (Ed. Code § 48918)
- The accused student has the right to confront the witnesses and evidence against her/him. (Ed. Code § 48918)

7

Who Gets Notice of Education Code Violations

Over the past few years the so-called "school-to-prison pipeline" has become an issue championed by groups across the political spectrum. The concern arises because, over the past ten to twenty years, schools across the country have increasingly involved law enforcement in incidents involving pupils which, in earlier years, would have been managed internally within the school through its own disciplinary system. Various causes of this increased criminalization of student behavior have been identified, but much of it has resulted from "zero tolerance" policies following tragic and extreme incidents such as the Columbine High School shooting. However, these "zero tolerance" policies have resulted in severe discipline, and even arrests, for innocent behaviors as districts abandoned the ability to apply common sense and to view incidents in their proper contexts.

Although there is no *legal* mandate or directive that California schools report, or not report, any crimes not covered by Section 48902, schools should adopt policies that balance the need to evaluate individual incidents to determine whether there is a need to involve law enforcement with the danger that such discretion can result, intentionally or not, in disparate negative impact on certain racial and socio-economic groups. Failure to assure equitable application of policies theoretically could result in litigation alleging discrimination, lack of equal protection and/or due process violations

Mandatory Reporting to Law Enforcement

California Code of Education section 48902 sets out which crimes a school district *must* report to law enforcement. These include assaults with deadly weapons, assaults with sufficient force likely to cause severe bodily injury, incidents involving the use, sale, possession, and distribution of illegal substances, alcohol, or imitation substances, and incidents involving a firearm or possession of explosives. Failure to report these crimes is an infraction and, conversely, reports made in good faith cannot result in civil liability.

Notification to Teachers

CA Education Code section 49079 (a) requires a school district to inform the teacher of each pupil who has engaged in, or is reasonably suspected to have engaged in, a conduct violation listed in 48900, except possession or use of tobacco or nicotine products. The district shall provide the information to the teacher based upon any records that the district maintains in its ordinary course of business, or receives from a law enforcement agency, regarding a pupil described in this section.

Any information received by a teacher pursuant to this section shall be received in confidence for the limited purpose for which it was provided and shall not be further disseminated by the teacher. The same information must be provided to the current teachers of any student who was suspended or expelled in another district and subsequently transfers into a new school district.

Part II
Special Education Discipline

8

Services During Short Term Suspensions

A student identified as an individual with disabilities pursuant to the Individuals with Disabilities Education Act (IDEA) is subject to the same grounds for suspension and expulsion that apply to students without disabilities. The basic difference between the discipline of a student with special needs and a general education student is that a student with special needs is entitled to certain procedural protections throughout the disciplinary process and when a change of placement is being contemplated.

A student with an IEP is treated the same as a general education student during the first ten (10) cumulative days of suspension. This means that a student with special needs is not entitled to IDEA protections for short term suspensions, until the eleventh (11th) school day of removal. An IEP team can decide to proactively hold an IEP meeting to examine the behavior leading to the short term suspensions during the first ten days, but the IDEA does not require such a meeting as part of the disciplinary procedural protections.

When a student with special needs is suspended for more than 10 cumulative school days in a school year, that student is entitled to continue to receive services, during the periods of suspension beyond ten days. For instance, a student with special needs has already been suspended for 9 cumulative days this school year and has engaged in a conduct violation for which she is going to be suspended for an additional 5 days. The additional 5 days will bring the student's cumulative suspensions for the year to 14 days. IDEA requires that starting on day 11 through day 14, the student receive services while suspended.

The services provided to the student during these four days must 1) enable the student to participate in the general curriculum; and 2) allow the student to make progress toward meeting the goals in the student's IEP. The student is not entitled to identical services to what she would have received if she were in school. The more services the student receives in her IEP, the more services she might need while suspended to meet the standard articulated above. For example, if the student was receiving resource services one hour per day, she might only need two total hours of home instruction during the four days in order to meet the legal standard. However, if she were in a self-contained SDC class with many other supports and services, the services she might need during the four day suspension to meet the legal standard may be one to two hours each of the four days. What those services will be during the short term suspension will be determined by appropriate school personnel in consultation with the teacher, and should be documented in the IEP and sent home to the parents of the student.

IDEA requires the principal or designee to monitor the number of days, **including portions of days**, that students with a valid IEP have been suspended during the school year to determine when the procedural protections are triggered and the students' right to services during suspension begins.

9

Manifestation Determination Procedures

Another disciplinary procedural safeguard provided by the IDEA is the requirement to conduct a manifestation determination within 10 school days of any decision to **change the placement** of a student with a disability because of a violation of a code of student conduct. It is important to remember that the requirement to conduct a manifestation determination when there is a proposed change in placement also applies to students with 504 Plans.

It is the decision to change the student's placement that triggers the requirement to conduct a manifestation determination. Therefore, the administrator must understand what proposed actions constitute a change in placement. IDEA defines a "change in placement" as either 1) a removal for more than 10 consecutive school days, or 2) a series of removals that constitute a pattern.

Change in Placement - Removal for More than 10 Consecutive School Days

The only way there can be a change in placement, in California, of a student with special needs based on a removal for more than 10 **consecutive** school days in the school year, is if the student is being recommended for expulsion or the student is facing a 45-day removal pursuant to IDEA special circumstances. In both instances, once the decision has been made to change the student's placement, the requirement to conduct the manifestation determination is triggered.

Change in Placement - Series of Removals That Constitute A Pattern

For there to be a change of placement based on a series of removals that constitute a pattern, all of the following three criteria must be met:
- The student has been removed for more than 10 **cumulative** school days in the school year;
- The removals are for behavior substantially similar; **and**
- The removals are in close proximity to one another. (The length and total amount of time of the removals are not relevant given California's suspension limitations.)

It is the administrator's responsibility to examine the above criteria and determine, on a case-by-case basis, whether there is a pattern of removals that constitute a change in placement. The best way to go about making this determination is for the administrator to consider the 10 cumulative days as a trigger to begin the analysis.

Once a student with special needs has reached 10 cumulative days of suspension in the school year, the administrator should review the previous suspensions that make up the 10 cumulative days and determine whether the behaviors are substantially similar. If the behaviors are **not** substantially similar, the analysis stops there, there is no change of placement based on a pattern, and a manifestation determination IEP is not required.

However, if the administrator examines the previous suspensions and finds that the behaviors are substantially similar, the administrator must then examine the proximity of the removals to one another. If the removals were spread out over the course of 6 months, the criteria is not met and it is not a change of placement, and a manifestation determination IEP is not required. If the removals all occurred within the course of a 6-week period, the proximity criteria would be met, and the administrator should determine that there has been a change in placement based on a pattern of removals, and a manifestation determination IEP would be required.

Manifestation Determination IEP

Once it has been determined that there is a proposed change in placement either because of an expulsion recommendation, 45 day removal, or a pattern of removals, a manifestation determination IEP must be held within 10 school days to determine whether the conduct is a manifestation of the student's disability.

The district, the parent, and relevant members of the IEP team must review all relevant information in the student's file: including the student's IEP, any teacher observations, and any relevant information provided by the parents. Once the above information has been reviewed, the IEP Team must discuss and answer the following questions:
- Whether the conduct in question was caused by, or had a direct and substantial relationship to, the student's disability; **or**
- Whether the conduct in question was the direct result of the District's failure to implement the IEP.

As these questions are being discussed by the IEP Team, it is important that the team clearly state the causal connection, or lack thereof, between the behavior and the disability or the specific elements of the IEP that were not implemented, if applicable, and how that failure led to the student's behavior. If either question is answered in the affirmative, the behavior is a manifestation of the disability and the proposed change in placement cannot go forward.

If the IEP Team determines that the behavior **was** a manifestation of the disability, the team must:
- Conduct a functional behavioral assessment, and implement a behavioral support plan (BSP or PBIP), provided the District had not previously conducted such assessment;
- Review the BSP or PBIP if the student already has such a plan, and modify it, as necessary, to address the behavior; and
- Except in special circumstances, return the student to the placement from which the student was removed, unless the parent and the District agree to a change of placement as part of the modification of the BSP or PBIP.

If the team determines that the behavior **was not** a manifestation of the disability, then the proposed change in placement may proceed:
- General education discipline procedures apply.
- Student may be suspended pending expulsion if expulsion is being recommended.
- Services may be provided in an interim alternative educational setting.
- The student should receive, *as appropriate*, a functional behavioral assessment, behavior intervention services and modifications, that are designed to address the behavior violation so that it does not recur

When there is a disciplinary change in placement following a determination that the student's behavior was not a manifestation of the disability or pursuant to a 45-day change in placement, the student is entitled to services beginning the 11th cumulative day of removal, as discussed in Services During Short Term Suspensions above. However, the services to be provided must be determined by the IEP Team.

10

Special Circumstances - 45-Day Placements

IDEA allows school personnel to remove a student with special needs to an interim alternative educational setting (IAES) for not more than 45 school days **without regard** to whether the behavior was a manifestation of the disability, when the student engages in the following conduct:

- Carries or possesses a weapon **to or at** school, **on** school premises, or **to or at** a school function;
- Knowingly possesses or uses illegal drugs, or sells or solicits the sale of a controlled substance, while **at** school, **on** school premises, or **at** a school function; or
- Inflicted serious bodily injury upon another person while **at** school, **on** school premises, **or** at a school function.

There are a few important things to note about this provision. First, the district's ability to utilize this provision for conduct that violates any of these sections is limited mostly to conduct that occurs at school or school functions. If the conduct involves a weapon, the district may also utilize this provision if the possession of the weapon occurs on the way to school. Practically speaking, the administrator must be able to establish that the conduct occurred within the applicable jurisdiction in order to remove a student with special needs to a 45-day interim placement for violation of any of these sections.

For example, if a fight that resulted in serious bodily injury occurred after school, off school grounds, the district would not be able to utilize the 45-day removal provision, as the conduct occurred outside of the jurisdiction for this section. The school could still suspend the student for the conduct pursuant to 48900(a)(1) & (2), and potentially recommend expulsion based on 48900(a)(1) & (2) and secondary findings, which are subject to the broader jurisdictional statement contained at 48900(s). However, if the IEP Team determined that the conduct was a manifestation of the student's disability, the expulsion process would stop and the student would be able to return to the placement from which s/he was removed.

Second, the 45-day removal provision is significant in that it is essentially sanctioned discrimination, as it allows a student with special needs who has engaged in one of the listed behaviors to be removed to an IAES for behavior that is a manifestation of the disability, without the consent of the parent. Using the same example above, let's say the fight occurred after school but on school grounds. The IEP team finds that the behavior is a manifestation of the disability, which would normally require that the student be returned to the placement from which s/he was removed. However, because the conduct occurred on campus, the 45-day removal provision can be utilized and the student can be placed in an IAES for up to 45 days, even though the behavior was a manifestation of the student's disability and the expulsion recommendation could not go forward.

Third, the basic assumptions that support using this process are: 1) the behavior is a manifestation of the disability, and 2) there is disagreement between the school and the parents about where the student should be placed following the conduct. Therefore, when utilizing the 45-day removal provision, it is important for the administrator to think about it as a time-out, an opportunity to have the student safely maintained in the IAES while the IEP Team explores alternative placement options that the parents can agree to. If it becomes apparent that the IEP Team cannot reach agreement about placement, the 45-day removal process allows the district and/or parents to pursue an administrative placement determination, while the student is still safely maintained in the IAES.

Lastly, because placement in the IAES is a change of placement, the location of the IAES and the services to be provided in the IAES must be determined by the IEP team. Additionally, the student should receive, *as* appropriate, a functional behavioral assessment, behavior intervention services, and modifications that are designed to address the behavior violation so that it does not recur.

11

Disciplinary Appeals

If the parents disagree with the IEP team's manifestation determination or disciplinary change in placement, they have a right to file a disciplinary appeal.

Similarly, if the district believes that maintaining the current placement of the student is substantially likely to result in injury to the student or others, the district has the right to file a disciplinary appeal.

Procedures

The appeals are filed with the Office of Administrative Hearings ("OAH") and are presided over by an Administrative Law Judge ("ALJ"). IDEA requires that the appeal be expedited, such that the hearing must occur within 20 school days of the date that the hearing is requested and the hearing decision must be rendered within 10 school days after the hearing has concluded. The student remains in the IAES pending the decision of the ALJ or until the expiration of the 45-day placement, whichever occurs first, unless the parent and the district agree otherwise.

Authority of the Hearing Officer

The ALJ hearing the disciplinary appeal has only two options when rendering a decision. The ALJ may order the return of the student to the placement from which the student was removed. This would mean that the ALJ found that the IEP Team's manifestation determination or placement decision was not appropriate or, if the appeal was filed by the district, that the district did not establish that it had done all it could to maintain the student safely in the student's original placement.

Alternatively, the ALJ may order a change of placement to the appropriate IAES for not more than 45 school days, if the ALJ determines that maintaining the current placement of the student is substantially likely to result in injury to the student or others. This would mean that the ALJ found that the determination of the IEP Team was appropriate or that the student could not be safely maintained in the original placement.

However, it is important to note that the authority of the ALJ to change a student's placement pursuant to a disciplinary appeal is limited to 45 days. Therefore, this is not a permanent solution to an IEP Team placement disagreement, because if the IEP Team cannot reach an agreement regarding placement prior to the expiration of the 45 days, the student has a right to return to the original placement from which s/he was removed.

12

Protections for Children Not Yet Eligible for Special Education

There is a group of general education students, who have not been identified as eligible for special education, who engage in conduct violations that could potentially lead to a change in placement (i.e. expulsion recommendation), and who are entitled to the procedural safeguard provided by IDEA.

Whether or not a particular student is entitled to the IDEA procedural safeguards will depend on whether the district may be deemed to have knowledge that the student was, or may be, a student with a disability at the time the student engaged the conduct violation. The determination of whether the district may be deemed to have knowledge it typically made by the school site administrator.

Is the District Deemed to Have Knowledge?

Below are the three criteria for determining whether the district may be deemed to have knowledge. I will first explain the criteria, then provide examples of each situation, then summarize the implications of what it means for a district to be deemed to have knowledge.

One, the parent of the student has expressed concern in writing, to supervisory or administrative personnel of the appropriate educational agency or to a teacher of the student, that the student is in need of special education. In this scenario, if the parent sent a letter, email, etc., to the student's teacher or a school administrator indicating that the parent believes that the student may need special education services, prior to the student engaging in the conduct violation, the district would be deemed to have knowledge.

Two, the parent of the student has requested a special education evaluation. In this scenario, the parent came into the office and asked the clerk what the process is for her to have her child assessed for special education. The clerk described the process and asked the parent to make her request in writing to start the process. Two weeks have passed and the parent has not turned in her written request for an evaluation, but her daughter has engaged in a conduct violation during this time and is facing an expulsion recommendation. In this scenario, the district would be deemed to have knowledge.

Third, the teacher of the student, or other personnel of the district, has expressed specific concerns about a pattern of behavior demonstrated by the student, directly to the director of special education or to other supervisory personnel. In this scenario, the school is holding an SST meeting for the student. During the meeting the teacher expresses specific concerns about the student's behavior in his class that the SST team tries to address with modifications and supports. Shortly following the meeting, the student engages in a conduct violation and is facing an expulsion recommendation. In this scenario, the district would be deemed to have knowledge.

Once the school administrator has been informed that there may be a basis of knowledge, s/he would be expected to investigate the allegation and, if substantiated, determine that there is a basis of knowledge and proceed to the next steps.

When a Basis of Knowledge Exists

It is important to note that a district being deemed to have knowledge is not a bad thing. If there is a basis of knowledge that the student was, or may have been a student with a disability at the time the student engaged in the conduct violation, then the student is entitled to special education protections. Practically speaking, all this means is that the school will need to jump through a few hoops before it can determine whether it has the authority to discipline the student.

Once a basis of knowledge has been established, the District must follow the steps below:
- Conduct an expedited comprehensive assessment (Ideally within 30 days);
- Hold an IEP to determine whether the student meets the IDEA eligibility criteria;
- If the student **is no**t eligible for special education, the IDEA process stops, the student is a general education student, and general education discipline procedures apply;

- If the student **is** eligible for special education, complete the development of the IEP and then conduct a manifestation determination based on the IEP just developed;
- If the behavior is found **to be a manifestation** of the student's disability, the general education disciplinary process stops and student is placed in the FAPE placement identified in the newly developed IEP and a functional behavioral assessment should be conducted to address the behavior at issue;
- If the behavior is found **not to be a manifestation** of the student's disability, the general education discipline procedures apply and the student may be disciplined for the conduct violation, subject to receiving continued educational services in the alternative setting.

Exceptions To There Being A Basis of Knowledge

There are three situations in which the district will not be deemed to have knowledge, regardless of whether any of the scenarios above have occurred. They are:
- The parent has not allowed an evaluation of the child;
- The parent has refused services; or
- The child has been evaluated and determined not to be a child with a disability. (This evaluation should have occurred within the calendar year)

These exceptions recognize that situations exist where the student has been evaluated and the parents have not allowed the district to properly serve the student. In these instances, the student would not be entitled to the IDEA protections and would be treated as a general education student for disciplinary purposes.

When There is Not A Basis of Knowledge

If the administrator, following an investigation into the matter, is unable to substantiate the allegation that the district has a basis of knowledge, then the student is a general education student and general education disciplinary procedures apply. However, IDEA requires that if the parent makes a request for an evaluation during the time period in which the student is subjected to disciplinary action, the evaluation must be conducted in an expedited manner. Pending the results of this evaluation, the child shall remain in the disciplinary educational placement determined by school authorities, and the outcome of the evaluation will not impact the previous discipline levied against the student.

Part III
Bullying and Protected Classes

13
Bullying in California — The Law

Bullying is a term that is widely used, with individuals attributing many different meanings to the word. It is used to refer to the conduct of a 1st grade boy who pulls the hair of a female classmate, to the conduct of a high school student who calls another student a derogatory name every time she sees that student, and everything in between. Many of the nationally available anti-bullying programs often describe bullying conduct as being "repeated over time," and involving an "imbalance of power."

While these are often characteristics of bullying, it is important for administrators and school staff to understand that California has a legal definition of bullying that does not require the conduct be "repeated over time," or involve an "imbalance of power." Therefore, it is imperative that school administrators understand the elements of California's "bullying" definition and the conduct that violates it.

CA Education Code Section 48900(r) defines bullying as:
- **Severe** <u>or</u> **pervasive physical** <u>or</u> **verbal** act or conduct, including communications made in <u>writing</u> or by means of an <u>electronic act</u>, and including one or more of the following:
    - Sex Harassment (48900.2)
    - Hate Violence (48900.3)
    - Threats, harassment, intimidation (48900.4)
- Has or is reasonably predicted to have one or more of the following:
    - Reasonable pupil in fear of <u>harm to person or property</u>
    - Reasonable pupil to experience <u>substantially detrimental effect to physical or mental health</u>

- o Reasonable pupil to experience <u>substantial interference with academic performance</u>
- o Reasonable pupil to experience <u>substantial interference with ability to participate in or benefit from services, activities, or privileges provided by the school</u>

Breaking this definition down into its three main sections will help better understand its elements.

- **Severe** <u>or</u> **pervasive physical** <u>or</u> **verbal** act or conduct, including communications made in <u>writing</u> or by means of an <u>electronic act</u>

The **first** section of the bullying definition describes the severity and nature of the bullying conduct. The use of the word "severe" suggests that the bullying conduct only needs to happen once, and if the conduct is severe enough, it would be sufficient to constitute bullying as defined in law. The bullying conduct can be physical, verbal, written or electronic. So, the first step in determining whether the conduct amounts to bullying, is to define the severity and nature of the conduct.

If the conduct is electronic, then the conduct is considered cyber-bullying. Cyber-bullying is the creation **or** transmission **originated on or off the schoolsite**, by means of an electronic device, including, but not limited to, a telephone, wireless telephone, or other wireless communication device, computer, or pager, of a communication, including, but not limited to, a message, text, sound, image, or a post on a social network internet web site. Cyber-bullying is bullying by an electronic act and all of the elements of the Bullying definition must be established just as if the bullying had occurred in person.

    … including one or more of the following:
- o Sex Harassment (48900.2)
- o Hate Violence (48900.3)
- o Threats, harassment, intimidation (48900.4)

The **second** section of the bullying definition requires that the bullying conduct violate one of these three existing sections in the Education Code. Specifically, it means that in California, for the underlying conduct to be considered bullying, it must be in the form of "Sexual Harassment," "Hate Violence," or "Threats, Harassment or Intimidation."

California Education Code defines each of the above sections as follows:

§48900.2 – Sexual Harassment

Unwelcome sexual advances, requests for sexual favors, and other verbal, visual, or physical conduct of a sexual nature, made by someone from or in the work or educational setting that is considered by a reasonable person of the same gender as the victim to be sufficiently severe or pervasive to have a negative impact upon the individual's academic performance or to create an intimidating, hostile, or offensive educational environment.

§48900.3 – Hate Violence

Caused, attempted to cause, threatened to cause, or participated in an act of hate violence. (Hate violence is violence directed toward an individual based on that person's membership to protected class. i.e. disability, gender, gender identity, gender expression, nationality, race or ethnicity, religion, sexual orientation, or association with a person or group with one or more of these actual or perceived characteristics.)

§48900.4 – Harassment, Threats, Intimidation

The pupil has intentionally engaged in harassment, threats, or intimidation, directed against school district personnel or pupils, that is sufficiently severe or pervasive to have the actual and reasonably expected effect of materially disrupting classwork, creating substantial disorder, and invading the rights of either school personnel or pupils by creating an intimidating or hostile educational environment.

So, the second step in determining whether the conduct amounts to bullying, is to examine the conduct and determine whether it meets the elements of one of the three definitions above.

Be aware that "Sexual Harassment," "Hate Violence," or "Threats, Harassment or Intimidation" are independent sections of the Education Code and, simultaneously, subsections of the Bullying definition. As independent sections of the Education Code, these sections only apply to students in grades 4-12. However, as a subsection of the Bullying definition, the California Department of Education ("CDE") has interpreted these sections to apply to all grades, K-12.

Practically, this means that if you are an administrator charging a 3rd grader with bullying based on conduct that amounts to sexual harassment, you can suspend the student for bullying by marking

48900(r) on the Notice of Suspension Form, but you would not be legally allowed to also check 48900.2, sexual harassment, on the Notice of Suspension form.

However, if you are an administrator charging an 8th grader with bullying based on conduct that amounts to sexual harassment, you can suspend the student for Bullying by marking 48900(r) on the Notice of Suspension Form, and you would, by definition, be required to also check 48900.2, sexual harassment, on the Notice of Suspension form. This is because any student grade 4-12 who violates the Bullying statute 48900(r), is by definition also violating either 48900.2 – Sexual Harassment, 48900.3 – Hate Violence, or 48900.4 – Threats, Harassment, or Intimidation.

- Has or is reasonably predicted to have one or more of the following:
    o Reasonable pupil in fear of harm to person or property
    o Reasonable pupil to experience substantially detrimental effect to physical or mental health
    o Reasonable pupil to experience substantial interference with academic performance
    o Reasonable pupil to experience substantial interference with ability to participate in or benefit from services, activities, or privileges provided by the school

The **third** and final section of the Bullying definition examines the impact that the bullying conduct had or could have reasonably been predicted to have on a "reasonable person," which often times is the victim.

Therefore, the final step in determining whether the conduct amounts to bullying, is to examine the impact of the conduct on a "reasonable person" and determine whether any of the negative impacts listed have occurred or could have reasonably been predicted to occur.

Education Code Section 48900(r)(3) defines "reasonable pupil" as a pupil, including, but not limited to, an exceptional needs pupil, who exercises average care, skill, and judgment in conduct for a person of his or her age, or for a person of his or her age with his or her exceptional needs. While it is arguable whether there is really such a thing as a "reasonable pupil," administrators are expected to consider what would be a reasonable response based on the severity and nature of the conduct, as well as the characteristics of the victim.

14

Transgender Students

Federal Law Protections

Historically, Title IX was interpreted to apply to sexual harassment and gender-based harassment claims. On April 29, 2014, the United States Department Of Education ("USDOE") clarified that the protections of Title IX of the Educational Amendments of 1972 extend to all students, regardless of sexual orientation or gender identity. This clarification provided unequivocal guidance that the Office For Civil Rights ("OCR") has the authority to investigate and enforce claims of discriminatory harassment based on gender identity.

California Law Protections

California law has prohibited discrimination and harassment based on gender identity for many years. However, because of the way the laws were drafted, it was unclear to many school administrators that gender identity and gender expression were among the protected categories. With the passage of AB 9 or "Seth's Law" on July 1, 2012, the law was clarified to include gender identity and gender expression explicitly in the list of protected categories. Seth's Law additionally instituted numerous procedural requirements for school districts, including but not limited to, modifying their nondiscrimination policies to identify gender identity and gender expression specifically as protected categories, and creating a complaint process to receive and investigate claims of harassment or discrimination based on a protected status.

In August 2013, the Governor signed Assembly Bill ("AB") 1266, the "School Opportunity and Success

Act," which became effective on January 1, 2014. This new law requires schools to allow students who identify as transgender to use school facilities and participate on sports teams (e.g., bathrooms, locker rooms) that correspond with their gender identity, providing further guidance to school administrators on how to respond to and support gender nonconforming students.

AB 1266 was written in response to statistics indicating that transgender youth are more likely than their non-transgendered peers to feel unsafe at school, making them three times more likely to miss a class or school day due to unsafe or uncomfortable conditions. The law was passed in an effort to make transgender youth feel safe at school and provide them with an equal learning opportunity.

Definitions

There are a number of relevant definitions that administrators should know as they navigate the various issues that arise around gender nonconforming students. These definitions are not meant to label any student, but are intended as functional descriptors. Students may or may not use these terms to describe themselves.

- Gender: Socially determined characteristics, roles, behaviors, and attributes a society expects from and considers appropriate for males and females; these characteristics are often referred to as "feminine" and "masculine." Under California law, "gender" is defined to include a person's gender identity. (Cal. Ed. Code § 210.7)

- Gender Expression: A person's gender-related appearance and behavior whether or not stereotypically associated with the person's assigned sex at birth (Cal. Ed. Code § 66260.7). It is the manner in which a person represents or expresses their gender to others, such as through their behavior, clothing, hairstyles, activities, voice or mannerisms.

- Gender Fluid: Persons who do not identify as, or who do not express themselves as, solely male or female.

- Gender Identity: A person's internal, deeply-rooted identification as male or female. All people have a gender identity, not just transgender people.

- Gender Nonconforming: Displaying gender traits that are not consistent with stereotypical characteristics associated with one's legal sex assigned at birth, or others' perceptions of that sex. This term can be used to describe people whose gender expression differs from stereotypical expectations about how boys and girls are "supposed to" look or act.

- <u>LGBTQ</u>: An umbrella term that stands for "lesbian, gay, bisexual, transgender, and questioning."

- <u>Sex</u>: The biological condition or quality of being a female or male human being.

- <u>Sexual Orientation</u>: A person's romantic or sexual attraction to people of the other and/or same gender. (Cal. Ed. Code § 212.6) Common terms used to describe sexual orientation include, but are not limited to, heterosexual, lesbian, gay, and bisexual. Sexual orientation and gender identity are different. Transgender students may identify as gay, lesbian, bisexual, or heterosexual.

- <u>Sexualized Bullying</u>: Unwanted or demeaning conduct or comments directed at or about an individual on the basis of actual or perceived gender, gender identity and expression, sex, sexual behavior, sexual orientation, or other related personal characteristics with the intention to humiliate. Anti-gay and sexist epithets are common forms of sexualized bullying.

- <u>Transgender</u>: A person whose sex at birth is inconsistent with who they know they are on the inside and with their gender expression.

- <u>Transition</u>: The process in which a person goes from living and identifying as one gender to living and identifying as another. This can include legal, medical and/or a social transition.

Practical Considerations For Schools When Supporting Gender Nonconforming Students

With the passage of AB 1266, Education Code 221.5(f) was amended to include the following language: "A pupil shall be permitted to participate in sex-segregated school programs and activities, including athletic teams and competitions, and use facilities consistent with his or her gender identity, irrespective of the gender listed on the pupil's records."

The below sections are intended to provide general guidance for school and district staff about how to address the needs of transgender and gender nonconforming students and how to respond in situations where questions arise about how to protect the legal rights or safety of students. These sections do not anticipate every situation that might occur with respect to transgender or gender nonconforming students. It is important to keep in mind that the needs of each student must be assessed on a case-by-case basis. In all cases, the goal is to ensure the safety, comfort, and healthy development of all students, including transgender students, maximizing inclusion and social integration while minimizing exclusion and stigmatization.

The responsibility for determining a student's gender identity rests with the student or, in the case of young students not yet able to advocate for themselves, with the parent or guardian.

A school should accept a student's asserted gender identity when there is evidence that it is a sincerely held part of the student's core identity. A school may not question or disregard the student's assertion of his or her gender identity unless school personnel have a credible basis for believing that the student is asserting a particular gender identity for some improper purpose.

Privacy Considerations

All persons, including students, have a right to privacy: the right to decide when, with whom, and how much highly personal information one wants to share about oneself to others. This includes the right to control dissemination of highly personal and private information such as one's transgender status or sexual orientation.

District and school personnel should not disclose a student's transgender status to others, including, but not limited to, other students, parents, or other school personnel, unless they are legally required to, the student has authorized such disclosure, or there is a specific and compelling "need to know" in order to protect the transgender student's interests. In those rare circumstances where disclosure is deemed to be absolutely necessary, before making any disclosure, school officials should inform the transgender student of the need to disclose and provide them with the opportunity and resources they may need to make the disclosure themselves.

District and school personnel may encounter situations where a transgender student has not disclosed their transgender status to their parents. Whenever possible, school administrators should speak with the student to confirm the manner in which the student will be referred to in conversation with the parent/guardian. Generally, when contacting the parent or guardian of a transgender student, school personnel should use the student's legal name and the gender pronoun that corresponds to the student's legal sex, unless the student, parent, or guardian has specified otherwise.

All students, including transgender students, have the right to openly discuss and express their gender identity or transgender status and to decide when, with whom, and how much to share that private information. In sharing this information, a student does not give up the right to privacy and at no time may the school use a student's self-disclosure as grounds for sharing information about the student's gender identity or transgender status without the student's permission.

Official Records

The District is required to maintain an official, permanent pupil record with the legal name and gender appearing on the student's birth certificate. On all other school-related records or documents, however, at the request of or with the consent of the student's parent/legal guardian (unless the student is over 18), schools should use a transgender student's requested name and gender pronoun. This would include physical records and documents, diplomas and other certificates of advancement, electronic records and documents, and school IDs. Every effort should be made to update student records with the student's requested name and gender pronoun or gender marker, and not to circulate records with the student's assigned birth name or gender marker. Schools should also identify routine areas where a transgender student's privacy could be violated by the improper usage of the legal name and gender marker. These include but are not limited to pre-printed labels, standardized tests, student IDs or library cards, lunch tickets, school photos, notices from the main office, attendance slips, grade books, posted lists of student names, lesson plans, seating charts and roll sheets used by substitute teachers, and any other places where students' names are commonly written.

In order to protect the student's privacy, and to prevent accidental disclosure of a student's transgender status, the school should maintain the official, permanent pupil record in a secure location, separate from the student's other records. If the official record is maintained electronically, similar security measures should be implemented to protect student privacy.

In the event that a student identifies as transgender, but is unable to obtain consent from a parent or legal guardian, a school administrator should meet with the student to discuss how the student would like to be addressed at school and implement a plan to ensure that the student's privacy is protected.

When a student or parent/legal guardian presents the school with documentation of a court-ordered legal name and/or gender change, the school must then change the official, permanent pupil record, to reflect the student's new legal name and gender.

Transgender students who transition after having graduated may ask their previous schools to amend school records or a diploma or transcript that include the student's birth name and gender. When requested, schools should amend the student's record, including reissuing a high school diploma or transcript, to reflect the student's current name and gender.

Names and Pronouns

Should a student or parent/legal guardian request to have the student addressed by a name and pronoun different from those associated with the student's sex at birth, the school must honor that request and set expectations accordingly. District and school officials may not require proof of a court-ordered name or gender change before honoring such a request. Districts and schools should also endeavor to proactively adapt student information systems to accommodate requested names and pronouns to prevent inadvertently revealing information that would violate the student's privacy.

While inadvertent slips or honest mistakes in the use of names or pronouns may occur, staff or students intentionally and persistently refusing to respect a student's gender identity by using the wrong name and gender pronoun is discriminatory and is a violation of the law.

Gender Segregated Activities

In situations where students are segregated by gender, such as for health education classes, students should be included in the group that corresponds to their gender identity.

Restroom Accessibility

Schools may maintain separate restroom facilities for male and female students. However, students shall have access to the restroom that corresponds to their gender identity.

Where available, a single stall, "gender neutral" restroom (such as in the health office) may be used by any student who desires increased privacy, regardless of the underlying reason. The use of such a "gender neutral" restroom shall be a matter of choice for a student and no student shall be compelled to use such a restroom.

As a proactive measure, administrators should take steps to identify private gender-neutral restrooms on their campus, as well as to de-stigmatize the use of such private options. Establishing clear guidelines and expectations with regards to students' physical privacy and boundaries is also important. Both can be reinforced through language in student handbooks, posted expectations, and through orientation and other processes for familiarizing students and guardians to the school and its facilities.

Locker Room Accessibility

Schools may maintain separate locker room facilities for male and female students. However, students shall have access to the locker room facility that corresponds to their gender identity.

If any student has a need or desire for increased privacy or safety, regardless of the underlying reason, they may be provided access to a reasonable alternative changing area or locker room such as:
- Use of a private area in the public area of the locker room facility (i.e., a nearby restroom stall with a door, an area separated by a curtain, or a P.E. instructor's office in the locker room).
- A separate changing schedule (either utilizing the locker room before or after other students).
- Use of a nearby private area (i.e., a nearby restroom or a health office restroom).

Use of such an alternative changing space shall be a matter of choice for a student and no student shall be compelled to use such an alternative. School administrators should also work to de-stigmatize the use of such options, as well as to establish clear guidelines and expectations with regard to respecting privacy and boundaries in changing areas and other close quarters.

Physical Education Classes and Intramural Sports

Transgender and gender nonconforming students shall be permitted to participate in physical education classes and intramural sports in a manner consistent with their gender identity.

Interscholastic Competitive Sports Teams

Transgender and gender nonconforming students shall be permitted to participate in interscholastic athletics in a manner consistent with their gender identity. (See CIF Bylaw 300-D.)

Dress Codes and School Uniform Policies

All students have the right to dress in accordance with their gender identity or gender expression. School dress codes and uniform policies should be gender-neutral, and should not restrict students' clothing choices on the basis of gender or traditional stereotypes about what males and females "should" wear.

Part IV
Miscellaneous Topics

15

Responding to Subpoenas For Student Records

The following is a general overall discussion of subpoenas and how to deal with them. Because there are many additional variations and potential issues, this discussion is not exhaustive. In specific cases, contacting the District's attorney may be necessary in order to ensure District compliance.

What is a subpoena?

A subpoena is document issued by one of the attorneys representing a party in a pending court or administrative proceeding commanding a designated individual to be present at a specific time or place. The majority of subpoenas the District receives are a type called a "subpoena duces tecum" which will direct a "custodian of the records" to bring to a court or administrative proceeding specified documents. A subpoena's format can vary greatly from one to another, but a subpoena always should contain the name of the proceeding, the court or administrative agency in which the proceeding is pending, the name and telephone number of the issuing attorney, and a case number.

How must a subpoena arrive at the District?

To be valid, a subpoena must be handed by an adult to the District staff member named on the subpoena or left at a District school site or office with an employee. This is called "service of the subpoena." Under most circumstances, a subpoena that arrives by fax, mail, or email attachment does not create a legal obligation on the part of the District to comply, because there is insufficient legal "service."

What if a subpoena arrives by fax, mail, or email attachment?

If a subpoena does arrive by means other than personal delivery, the District should contact the lawyer whose name appears on the document and indicate that although copy of subpoena made its way to the District, there was no personal delivery so no documents will be produced. Although there is no duty to respond to a subpoena that is not personally delivered, the prudent course is to check with the lawyer who issued the subpoena to confirm the District's understanding of how the subpoena arrived and prevent any enforcement proceedings against the District in court based on inaccurate or false statements. The District should also expect that an attorney who tried to serve a subpoena by some "short cut," thinking the District would simply provide the requested documents, will re-serve the subpoena correctly.

What should be done with a subpoena?

The District should develop a procedure, distributed to all employees who are in positions with public access, whether at a school site or the District Office, to have one designated administrator in the District, and in each department involved, notified if a subpoena shows up, either properly served personally or otherwise, to ensure no District default regarding subpoenas. As part of whatever policy the District develops, a copy should go also to the District employee whose name appears on the document. Most often, however, the subpoena will not name a particular person, but require a particular department head or a "custodian of the records" of a specific category of documents. This person should receive a copy of the subpoena and promptly prepare the response by gathering the documents listed. Whether the documents requested are financial information, staff records, cumulative files, student discipline records, attendance data, special education files, or other records, the subpoena should go to the appropriate department administrator. Note that in some cases with multiple categories of records, more that one District administrator should receive a copy. This is a sound reason for having a District-wide policy in effect to keep track of District compliance with subpoenas.

What if there is not enough time to assemble all of the documents by the date required in the subpoena?

Often, there is a very short time within which to provide subpoenaed documents. Therefore, it is important to begin immediate efforts to respond to a subpoena when it arrives. Sometimes, however, there will not be enough time to locate and assemble requested documents. Just as in the situation where the subpoena arrives by means other than personal delivery, the lawyer who issued the subpoena should be contacted if enough time is not available to comply. The issuing attorney can agree with the District to alter the terms of the subpoena. Make certain that the attorney confirms any agreement in writing. If the lawyer refuses to be reasonable, the administrator who is the "custodian of the records," should state, with particulars, what the problem is and submit a declaration as part of a Motion for In Camera Review and for Protective Order, as discussed below. In the case of insufficient time, the District should at least have this Motion on file with the court to prevent any adverse legal consequences.

What documents should be assembled to comply with a subpoena?

All documents reasonably included in the category of records identified in a subpoena should be located and gathered together. Documents may be in paper files, in photographs, audio recordings, or maintained on electronic media. This may require going to several sources, plus downloading emails or data in computer files. If there are no District records reasonably included in a category listed in a subpoena, that fact should be noted also.

Once the documents are assembled, what happens to them?

Once gathered, the assembled documents are copied. The District should have one set to keep with its files to show exactly what was produced. The other copy should go into a large envelope bearing the District's name, the proceeding, and the case number as appears on the subpoena.

Must the District administrator deliver the documents personally?

Unless a subpoena expressly requires testimony from a District administrator or employee, the documents may be sent to the location noted on the subpoena accompanied by a declaration signed by the administrator who oversaw the assembly of the documents as the "custodian of the records." This declaration is the equivalent of sworn testimony stating that the documents are from the District's files and were prepared by District staff as part of the regular and customary process of making such records. A form for this declaration often accompanies a subpoena. The District's counsel can assist in preparing the declaration. This signed declaration is attached to the documents placed in the envelope containing the assembled documents. Seal the envelope and attach another copy of the declaration to the outside. The entire package is then most often combined with a Motion, as described below, and sent or delivered to the location on the subpoena (NOT to the lawyer who issued the subpoena) far enough in advance to arrive on time.

How does the District protect confidential information?

Most often, District files required to comply with a subpoena are pupil records or human resources information pertaining to a particular staff member. The District has a clear legal duty to prevent disclosure of these records to unauthorized individuals. The law, however, also obligates the District to produce documents listed in a lawful subpoena. To resolve this legal conflict and meet each of these legal duties, the District may refer the issue to the District's attorney to prepare a "Motion for In Camera Review and Protective Order." This is a request from the District to the judge presiding over the proceeding to keep the District's records from disclosure until the judge has reviewed them privately. The Motion asks the judge to keep the documents under seal, and to release only those records the judge deems necessary to the case, and then require whoever sees the released records to be bound by a court order to keep them confidential or otherwise be in contempt of court and subject to punishment.

What must the District do if pupil records are sought?

As soon as a subpoena is received asking for pupil records, the District must send a letter to the parents or guardians of the pupils involved disclosing the receipt of the subpoena, the District's intention to comply with the law and turn over the documents. A telephone call in addition is good practice to be certain the parents are aware of the subpoena. In the letter, the parents are to be informed of the time and place the records will be turned over and that they can seek legal counsel to object to the release of the records. The District should exercise care to be certain that the parents of all pupils whose identifiable information is in a subpoena request receive this notice. Often, the requested records of one student will include references to other District students.

If a motion is warranted, what must the District do?

When the District prepares confidential documents in answer to a subpoena and the District's counsel drafts a Motion, at the time and location on the subpoena for bringing in the documents, the District's attorney will be present to file the motion and state the District's position. Alternatively, the District can have an administrator appear or leave the matter for the judge to decide based on the package of documents with the declaration and written Motion and with no District representative present. In any case, the Motion with a copy of the Declaration (without the documents) must be sent to the lawyer who issued the subpoena as well as any other lawyers in the case. The attorney who issued the subpoena should be able to provide the names and addresses of the other lawyers involved. Often, a subpoena is issued by a deputy public defender. In this instance, the opposing counsel is most likely in the district attorney's office.

16

Counseling Records and Confidentiality

Educational counseling is a specialized service provided by a school counselor possessing a valid credential with a specialization in pupil personnel services who is assigned specific times to directly counsel pupils. Ed. Code § 49600, subd. (a).

Section 49600 of the Education Code codifies that educational counseling includes, but is not limited to: academic counseling, career and vocational counseling, and personal and social counseling. In providing academic counseling, a school counselor should discuss, at minimum: "establishment and implementation with parental involvement of the pupil's immediate and long-range educational plans;" "optimizing progress towards achievement of proficiency standards;" completion of the required curriculum in accordance with the pupil's needs, abilities, interests, and aptitudes;" and "Academic planning for access and success in higher education programs including advisement on courses needed for admission to public colleges and universities, standardized admissions tests, and financial aid." § 49600(b)(1)(A)-(D).

In providing career and vocational counseling, a school counselor should assist the student in: "planning for the future;" "becoming aware of their career potential;" "developing realistic perceptions of work;" and "relating to the work world." § 49600(b)(2)(A)-(D). Finally, personal and social counseling should focus on fostering interpersonal relationships to promote "development of their academic abilities, careers and vocations, personalities, and social skills." §49600(c).

Confidentiality of Information Received During Counseling

California law strictly protects the confidentiality of personal information shared by a student while receiving counseling from a school counselor. Any information of a personal nature disclosed by a pupil 12 years of age or older in the process of receiving counseling from a school counselor, and any information of a personal nature disclosed to a school counselor by the pupil's parent or guardian, is confidential. Ed. Code § 49602. In other words, not all information is confidential, only such information that is "of a personal nature," disclosed by a student 12 years of age or older, or a student's parents, "in the process of receiving counseling from a school counselor." While this section does not define "information of a personal nature," it does codify that such information does not "include routine objective information related to academic and career counseling."

The information may not be revealed, released, discussed, or referred to by the school counselor except that such information may be shared: with psychotherapists, other health care providers, or the school nurse solely for purposes of referring the student for treatment; with local child protective agencies to report of child abuse or neglect; with the principal or parents when the school counselor has reasonable cause to believe that disclosure is necessary to avert a clear and present danger to the health, safety, or welfare of the pupil, administrators, teachers, school staff, parents, pupils, and other school community members; with the principal or other school personal, and, as necessary, the parents and other persons outside the school, when the pupil indicates that a crime, involving the likelihood of personal injury or significant or substantial property losses, will be or has been committed; and, with persons specified in a written waiver of confidentiality after this written waiver of confidence is read and signed by the student and maintained in the pupil record file. Ed. Code §49602(a)-(e).

School counselors must be careful not to disclose confidential information without consent or pursuant to a statutory exception. While the issue has not been addressed in California, several other jurisdictions have found that school counselors were personally liable for damages pursuant to a §1983 claim or common law tort claim, for disclosing confidential information.

The remaining paragraphs of Section 49602 further codify the purpose and extent of such confidentiality. While school counselors do not enjoy any doctor-patient privilege between themselves and the students they counsel, the Legislature created a "privilege of confidentiality under this section to assist the pupil whenever possible to communicate more effectively with parents, school staff, and others." Furthermore, Section 49602 specifically disallows disclosure of confidential information shared during a counseling session to the student's parents "when the school counselor has reasonable cause to believe that the disclosure would result in a clear and present danger to the health, safety, or welfare of the pupil." On the other hand, section 49602 requires a school counselor to "disclose information deemed to be confidential pursuant to this section to law enforcement agencies when ordered to do so by order of a court of law, to aid in the investigation of a crime, or when ordered to testify in any administrative or judicial proceeding." Such confidentiality also does not "limit the counselor from conferring with other school staff, as appropriate, regarding modification of the pupil's academic program."

Most importantly, the remaining paragraphs of section 49602 codify: "No person required by this section to keep information discussed during counseling confidential shall incur any civil or criminal liability as a result of keeping that information confidential." However, a school counselor could potentially face liability for failing to disclose such confidential information when there is a mandatory reporting requirement.

17

Home Schooling and Attendance

Students are increasingly being home schooled in California. School administrators need to be aware of the legal authority that allows students to be home schooled and the documentation that must be provided to the school to allow the student's exemption from compulsory attendance laws.

Education Code section 48222 allows a child to be educated at home and be exempted from the compulsory attendance law otherwise requiring participation in the District's program. The District therefore can permit this attendance exemption and drop a student under section 48222 after receiving the required affidavit.

Compulsory attendance exemptions are granted:

> "…only after verification by the attendance supervisor of the district, or other person designated by the board of education, that the private school has complied with the provisions of Section 33190 requiring the annual filing by the owner or other head of a private school of an affidavit or statement of prescribed information with the Superintendent of Public Instruction. The verification required by this section shall not be construed as an evaluation, recognition, approval, or endorsement of any private school or course."

There is no specific provision in the Education Code for home schooling, but CDE recognizes instruction of a single student at home after the filing of this affidavit as a "private school." CDE requires these affidavits to be filed in the first two weeks of October of each year and the affidavit must contain all of the information listed in Education Code section 33190, as contained in the line items on the affidavit.

Section 48222 also requires teaching in English, following the same curriculum as the public schools, and keeping attendance records, because to justify an exemption from the compulsory education statutes the instruction must be full-time:

> *"[The private or home] school shall . . . be taught in the English language and shall offer instruction in the several branches of study required to be taught in the public schools of the state. The attendance of the pupils shall be kept by private school authorities in a register, and the record of attendance shall indicate clearly every absence of the pupil from school for a half day or more during each day that school is maintained during the year."*

As an assistance to home schooling parents developing course content, CDE refers them to its "Standards and Frameworks" web page. If the parent requests the cum file, in writing, this should be treated as any pupil records request and provided within five school days. It is recommended that a duplicate file be maintained by the District for the pupil in case the s/he returns to the District. So long as the pupil resides within the District's boundaries, s/he must be re-enrolled in the District at the parents' request.

18

Disruptive Parents

Increasingly, situations have arisen where parents of students have entered a school campus or school sponsored activity and have engaged in disruptive and/or intimidating behavior. It is important for administrators to be aware of the laws that govern disruptive parent behavior and the administrator's authority to address it.

School districts have the legal obligation to maintain order and safety within the district's schools, buildings, grounds, and facilities, and at all times must protect the health and safety of staff and students. This mandatory duty extends to all school activities and sponsored events.

State law prohibits any person from coming onto public school property and willfully interfering with the discipline, good order, lawful conduct, or administration of any school activity, with the intent to disrupt, obstruct, or inflict damage to property or bodily injury upon any person. Education Code section 44810. Violators of this provision face potential punishment of fines of at least five hundred to one thousand dollars or imprisonment up to one year. Any parent, guardian, or other individual who materially disrupts extracurricular activities, or causes substantial disorder is guilty of a misdemeanor and may be fined up to one thousand dollars or imprisonment for one year, or both. Education Code section 44811. Additionally, Education Code section 32210 deems one who willfully disturbs a public school or public school meeting guilty of a misdemeanor punishable by a fine of up to five hundred dollars.

The law further empowers the District to notify a person that consent for that person to be on school property has been withdrawn whenever there is a reasonable cause to believe that the person has willfully disrupted the orderly operation of the campus. Penal Code sections 626.4, *et seq*. Under these criminal law provisions, should a person who has been notified that consent to be on campus has been withdrawn and willfully enters or remains on the campus is guilty of a misdemeanor, and may be fined up to five hundred dollars, or imprisoned up to six months, or both.

Appendix

Appendix A
Glossary of Discipline Definitions

Glossary of Discipline Definitions

"Hearsay"

A statement made out of court that is offered in court, by someone other than the declarant, as evidence to prove the truth of the matter asserted – secondhand information.

"Direct Evidence"

Evidence offered by someone with firsthand knowledge of the event.

"Percipient Witness"

A witness who has firsthand knowledge of the event. *A subpoena can only be issued to compel the personal appearance of a percipient witness.

"Firearm"
Any device, designed to be used as a weapon, from which is expelled through a barrel a projectile by the force of any explosion or other form of combustion.
Penal Code sec. 12001(b).

"Self-Defense"
Free from fault (no provocation), no convenient mode of escape by retreat or declining the combat, and present impending peril creating a reasonable belief of necessity.

"Serious physical injury" - 48915 (a) (1) definition

Serious physical impairments of physical condition, such as loss of consciousness, concussion, bone fracture, protracted loss or impairment of function of any bodily member or organ, a wound requiring suturing, and serious disfigurement. [Title 5, Section 11993(q).]

Special Education Discipline Definitions

"Dangerous Weapon"

The IDEA allows districts to remove a student to an interim alternative educational setting for up to 45 school days for carrying or possessing a weapon. According to both IDEA '97 and IDEA '04, the term "'weapon' has the meaning given the term '**dangerous weapon**' under Section 930(g)(2) of Title 18, United States Code."

The section, in turn, states: "The term '**dangerous weapon**' means a weapon, device, instrument, material, or substance, animate or inanimate, that is used for, or is readily capable of, causing death or serious bodily injury, except that such term does not include a pocket knife with a blade of less than 2 1/2 inches in length.

"Serious Bodily Injury" (Special education 45-day placement definition)
– means bodily injury that involves-
(A) a substantial risk of death;

(B) extreme physical pain;

(C) protracted and obvious disfigurement; or

(D) protracted loss or impairment of the function of a bodily member, organ, or mental faculty

18 U.S.C. § 1365(h)(3)

"Change of Placement" (special education)
1) More than 10 consecutive school days; or
2) Pattern
   Total more than 10 school days in the school year;
   Behavior substantially similar; **and**
   Additional factors, length, total amount of time, proximity of removals to each other.
(Determined by LEA on case-by-case basis)

Appendix B
Student Statement Form

STUDENT STATEMENT FORM

School Name _____ Date: _____ Student #: _____

SWORN DECLARATION OF _____
Print student name

I, _____ , declare the following:

_____
_____
_____
_____
_____
_____
_____
_____
_____
_____
_____
_____
_____
_____
_____
_____
_____
_____

I have read this declaration and do declare under penalty of perjury and the laws of the State of California that it is true and correct to the best of my knowledge.

Dated: _____
Signature

Appendix C
Sworn Declaration of Witness

SWORN DECLARATION OF WITNESS
Education Code Section 48918, Subsection (f)
(Unreasonable risk of harm)

In matter of the suspension and possible expulsion of _____

a student enrolled at _____ school. I, _____,

feel the disclosure of my identity as a witness and my testimony as a witness at the hearing

would subject me to unreasonable risk of psychological or physical harm.

NARRATIVE: (Explain the unreasonable risk of psychological or physical harm)

_____
_____
_____
_____
_____
_____
_____
_____

I declare under penalty of perjury that the foregoing is true and correct this

day _____ month _____, year _____

Declarant Signature: _____

Appendix D
Notice of Suspension Form

********* School District
(School address)

Notification of Administrative Suspension from School

Date	School		Student's Phone Number		
Student's Name:	Last	First	Grade	Student ID	Birthdate
Suspension From: Day	Time	Date / /	Suspension Code:	Special Ed Student ☐Yes ☐No	
Day Return:	Time	Date / /	**Police Report** ☐N/A ☐Pending ☐Filed #	**Expulsion Review** ☐N/A ☐Recommended ☐Pending	

EDUCATION CODE SECTION 48900
- ☐ a.1. Caused, attempted to cause, or threatened to cause physical injury.
- ☐ a.2. Willfully used force or violence on another person, except in self defense.
- ☐ b. Possessed, sold or otherwise furnished any firearm, knife, explosive, or other dangerous object. ++
- ☐ c. Possessed, used, sold, furnished, or been under the influence of any controlled substance, alcohol, or intoxicant. ++
- ☐ d. Offered, arranged, or negotiated to sell a controlled substance, alcohol or intoxicant and then provided a replica substance. ++
- ☐ e. Attempted or committed robbery or extortion.
- ☐ f. Attempted or caused damage to school or private property.
- ☐ g. Attempted or stole school or private property.
- ☐ h. Possessed, or used a tobacco product.
- ☐ i. Committed an obscene act or engaged in habitual profanity or vulgarity.
- ☐ j. Possessed, offered, arranged, or negotiated to sell drug paraphernalia.
- ☐ k. Disrupted school activities or defied school personnel.
- ☐ l. Knowingly received stolen school or private property.
- ☐ m. Possessed an imitation firearm.++ - **if fires metallic projectile**
- ☐ n. Attempted or committed sexual assault or committed a sexual battery. ++
- ☐ o. Harassed, threatened, or intimidated a student complainant or witness in a school disciplinary matter.
- ☐ p. Unlawfully offered, arranged to sell, negotiated to sell, or sold the prescription drug Soma. ++
- ☐ q. Engaged in, or attempted to engage in, hazing.
- ☐ r. Engaged in an act of bullying, including electronic means ☐ 48900.2 ☐ 48900.3 ☐ 48900.4 (indicate which was violated)
- ☐ t. A pupil who aids or abets in the attempted or infliction of physical injury to another.
- ☐ .2 Committed sexual harassment. (Gr.4-12)
- ☐ .3 Attempted, threatened, caused, or participated in hate violence. (Grades 4-12)
- ☐ .4 Created an intimidating or hostile educational environment. (Gr.4-12)
- ☐ .7 Made terroristic threats against school officials or property.

++ Indicates law enforcement MUST be notified

MANDATORY RECOMMENDATION FOR EXPULSION
(Education Code 48915(c)):
- ☐ c.1. Sale, possession or furnishing a firearm. ++
- ☐ c.2. Brandishing a knife at another person. ++
- ☐ c.3. Selling a controlled substance. ++
- ☐ c.4. Sexual assault or sexual battery. ++
- ☐ c.5. Possession of an explosive. ++

DISCRETIONARY MANDATORY RECOMMENDATION FOR EXPULSION
(Education Code 48915 (a)(1):
- ☐ 1.A Causing serious injury to another person, except in self-defense.++
- ☐ 1.B Possession of a knife, or other dangerous object of no reasonable use to the pupil.++
- ☐ 1.C Unlawful possession of any controlled substance except for the first offense for the possession of not more than one avoirdupois ounce of marijuana, other than concentrated cannabis, over the counter medications, or prescribed medication.++
- ☐ 1.D Robbery or extortion.
- ☐ 1.E Assault or battery on any school employee.++

Parent Conference ☐ Held ☐ Requested ☐ Via Phone
Date:_____ Time:_____
Contact Name:_____

Student Conference ☐ Held ☐ Postponed until _____
Date:_____ Time:_____

Total Days Suspended in the School Year: _____

Factual explanation of incident(s): Date:_____ Time: _____
Location: ☐ On Campus ☐ Off Campus ☐ School activity off school grounds ☐ Attendance related
_____

Dear Parents/Guardians:

This suspension is in compliance with Education Code Section 48900 and 48915 et seq. The suspension has been discussed with your student and he/she has been given an opportunity to explain his/her side of the incident.* If a conference has been requested, please make every effort to attend. Under state law, you are required to respond to this request without delay. If you wish, you and your student may review his/her record as provided in Education Code 49069. Make-up work and/or tests may be provided for your student, if requested, for the period of suspension.

If you feel the suspension is inappropriate and have discussed your concerns with the school principal, you may appeal the suspension to (Name of appropriate person), Assistant Superintendent. Call the Educational Services Department, (***-****) for an appointment.

PLEASE NOTE: During the school day, your student must not be on or near any school campus. Supervision is the responsibility of the parent/guardian during the suspension.

By:_____
      Principal/Designee

*The principal or designee may suspend a student without a conference if an emergency situation exists.
State laws allow the principal to recommend suspension for violations of Education Code section 48900 subdivisions (a), (b), (c), (d), (e), and other subdivisions upon a first offense, if the pupil's presence is deemed to be a danger to persons.

© 2015 The Law Office of Dora J. Dome

Appendix E
Letter Extending Suspension

[DISTRICT LETTERHEAD]

LETTER EXTENDING SUSPENSION
PENDING EXPULSION

[Date]

[Address]

Re: [Student's Name]
     [Student's Birth Date]

Dear _____:

    The principal of [School Name] has recommended the expulsion of your [son/daughter/grandson/granddaughter], [Student's Name]. The Education Code sections on student suspension and expulsion were explained to you and [Student] during a meeting held in [Teacher/Administrator's Name] office on [Date]. The expulsion process follows the law as outlined by the Education Code.

    The incident of [Date], described in the attached Notice, demonstrates a clear breach of discipline and defiance of school rules and regulations by [Student's Name]. Therefore, I am extending the suspension until a decision on expulsion is reached by the Board of Education.

    I have determined that [Student's] presence at school would [cause a danger to persons or property and/or cause disruption of the instructional process]; therefore, [Student] is to remain away from school at all times during this suspension period. Arrangements for obtaining classwork to be completed at home may be made with [Student's] counselor or school administrator. Supervision of the pupil during the suspension is the responsibility of the parent or guardian.

    It is important that you and [Student] meet with [Teacher or Administrator] as soon as possible to discuss the Statement of Charges and the hearing process. Please call [Enter phone number] to make an appointment.

                                      Sincerely,

                                       [Signature]
                                     [Title]

cc:

Appendix F
Letter Extending Suspension.IDEA

[Date]

[Address]

Re: [Student's Name]
[Student's Birth Date]

Dear _____:

The principal of [School Name] has recommended the expulsion of your [son/daughter/grandson/granddaughter], [Student's Name]. [Student] is a student with a disability pursuant to the IDEA. Therefore, before expulsion proceedings can be considered, [Student] is entitled to have an IEP team meeting within ten (10) school days of the date of suspension to determine whether there is a relationship between the reported misconduct and [Student's] disability.

The Education Code sections on student suspension and expulsion were explained to you and [Student] during a meeting held in [Teacher/Administrator's Name] office on [Date]. The expulsion process follows the law as outlined by the Education Code.

The incident of [Date] demonstrates a clear breach of discipline and defiance of school rules and regulations by [Student's Name]. Therefore, I am extending the suspension pending expulsion and until the IEP team has determined whether there is a relationship between the misconduct and [Student's] disability. If the IEP team determines that there is not a relationship between the conduct and [Student's] disability, the suspension will continue until a decision on expulsion is reached by the Board of Education.

I have determined that [Student's] presence at school would [cause a danger to persons or property and/or cause disruption of the instructional process]; therefore, [Student] is to remain away from school at all times during this suspension period. Beginning on the eleventh day of removal in a school year, [Student's] IEP will be implemented to the extent necessary to enable [him/her] to appropriately progress toward achieving the goals set out in [Student's] IEP, as determined by the IEP team.

Sincerely,

[Signature]
[Title]

Appendix G
Letter Terminating Expulsion.IDEA

[Date]

[Address]

        Re: [Student's Name]
                [Student's Birth Date]

Dear _____:

     The IEP team met on [Date] and determined that there was a relationship between the reported misconduct and [Student's] disability. Therefore, all disciplinary action will be terminated and [Student] will be returned to his/her previous placement.

.

                         Sincerely,

                         [Signature]
                         [Title]

Appendix H
Expulsion Packet Checklist

Expulsion Packet Checklist

_____ Notice of Suspension Form

_____ Principal Summary/Recommendation For Expulsion

_____ Letter Extending Suspension Pending Expulsion

_____ Notice of Hearing and Charges Letter

_____ Incident Report(s)/ Witness Statements (Staff and students) (Redacted)

_____ Evidence (Photos, weapon, police reports, medical records, etc)

_____ Interventions AND Discipline History

_____ Student Status reports

_____ Grade Reports/ Transcripts/Attendance

_____ Request for Continuance, if applicable

Appendix I
Expulsion Hearing List of Exhibits

INDEX OF ATTACHMENTS INCLUDED IN THE RECOMMENDATION FOR EXPULSION OF

STUDENT NAME

CASE NO.

BEFORE THE [BOARD OF EDUCATION or ADMINISTRATIVE HEARING PANEL]

DATE

Document Title	Page
Suspension Letter & Notice of Suspension	
Principal's Recommendation For Expulsion	
Director's Notice of Meeting to Consider Extension of Suspension Letter	
Director's Notice of Extension of Suspension	
Notification of Recommendation for Expulsion and Expulsion Hearing	
Student Declaration	
Victim/Witness Statements	
Photograph of Item in Student's Possession	
Student Discipline Report: Referrals/Suspensions	
School Attendance Record & Truancy Documentation	
Remediation & Support Services Provided Student	
Teachers' Progress Reports	
Transcript Of Student's Grades	
Board Policy	**Appendix**
Copy Of Education Code 48900 & 48915 (Student Services)	
Copy Of School Rules & District Discipline Policy (Student Services)	

Appendix J
Stipulated Expulsion

Stipulation and Request for Waiver of Expulsion Hearing with Recommendation for Expulsion

To: ********, Superintendent
********** Unified School District

Re: Name of Student
School
Principal Recommending Expulsion

[Student Name Full], student, and [Parent Name], parent of student, acknowledge meeting with [Special Education Director or designee] on [meeting date]. We have been informed of and understand the right to due process with regard to the expulsion recommendation against [name of student] by [name of principal], of the ******** Unified School District.

Moreover, we received a copy of the Notice of Expulsion and Charges dated [Charge ltr date] and understand the contents of that notice.

We understand that the expulsion hearing has been scheduled for [Day/Date of Hearing], at [Time], in the [Name of District Office], located at [Address of District Office], California. In particular, we have been informed and understand that we have the right to a full evidentiary hearing, the right to appear in person or employ and be represented by counsel at this hearing, the right to inspect and obtain copies of all documents to be used at the hearing, the right to confront and question all witnesses who testify at the hearing, the right to question all evidence presented, and to present oral and documentary evidence on [student's name]'s behalf, including witnesses. We have received a written copy of these rights. We have also received a written description of the charges that led to the recommendation for expulsion, copies of applicable provisions of the California Education Code and District Rules and Regulations governing expulsions.

We stipulate and agree that [name of student] is subject to expulsion from the District for having committed acts in violation of Education Code section _____ [description of statutory offense]. [If required by Education Code section 48915] We further stipulate that other means of correction are not feasible or have repeatedly failed to bring about proper conduct or that due to the nature of the violation, the presence of the pupil causes a continuing danger to the physical safety of the pupil or others.

After careful consideration, we voluntarily request a waiver of the expulsion hearing before the ******** Unified School District Hearing Panel, located at [address]. We understand that the purpose and function of the waived hearing would have been for fact-finding and to submit recommendations to the Board of Education when the Board meets to deliberate and act on this matter. In addition to waiving the expulsion hearing, we also request that all legal time lines in this matter be waived.

We understand that an expulsion recommendation will be submitted to the Board of Education for its review and final action. The District administration will recommend that [student's name] be expelled for [one/two semester(s)], through [date].

We understand that the Board of Education will ensure that an education program is provided to [student's name] for the period of the expulsion. In addition we understand that the Board of Education will recommend a plan of rehabilitation for [student's name]. This rehabilitation plan may include, but not be limited to, periodic review as well as assessment at the time of review for readmission. The plan may also include recommendations for improved academic performance, tutoring, special education assessments, job training, counseling, employment, community service, or other rehabilitative programs.

We understand that at the conclusion of [student's name] expulsion term, [he/she] shall be reviewed for readmission to a school maintained by the District or to the school [student's name] last attended. Upon completion of the readmission process, the Board of Education will readmit [name of student], unless the Board of Education makes a finding that the pupil has not met the conditions of [his/her] rehabilitation plan or continues to pose a danger to campus safety or to other pupils or employees of the District.

By requesting this Waiver of Hearing on Expulsion, we acknowledge that, should the Board of Education vote not to accept the administration's recommendation, we retain the right to withdraw this Waiver of Expulsion Hearing and have the matter heard by the ******** Unified School District Hearing Panel

EXPULSION REHABILITATION PLAN:

[ADD TERMS OF REHAB PLAN]

[Name of Student]   Date

[Parent]   Date

[Parent]   Date

Appendix K1-8
Relevant C.F.R.
Special Education Discipline

Code of Federal Regulations
 Title 34. Education
  Subtitle B. Regulations of the Offices of the Department of Education
   Chapter III. Office of Special Education and Rehabilitative Services, Department of Education
    Part 300. Assistance to States for the Education of Children with Disabilities (Refs & Annos)
     Subpart E. Procedural Safeguards
      Discipline Procedures

34 C.F.R. § 300.530

§ 300.530 Authority of school personnel.

Effective: October 13, 2006

Currentness

(a) Case-by-case determination. School personnel may consider any unique circumstances on a case-by-case basis when determining whether a change in placement, consistent with the other requirements of this section, is appropriate for a child with a disability who violates a code of student conduct.

(b) General.

(1) School personnel under this section may remove a child with a disability who violates a code of student conduct from his or her current placement to an appropriate interim alternative educational setting, another setting, or suspension, for not more than 10 consecutive school days (to the extent those alternatives are applied to children without disabilities), and for additional removals of not more than 10 consecutive school days in that same school year for separate incidents of misconduct (as long as those removals do not constitute a change of placement under § 300.536).

(2) After a child with a disability has been removed from his or her current placement for 10 school days in the same school year, during any subsequent days of removal the public agency must provide services to the extent required under paragraph (d) of this section.

(c) Additional authority. For disciplinary changes in placement that would exceed 10 consecutive school days, if the behavior that gave rise to the violation of the school code is determined not to be a manifestation of the child's disability pursuant to paragraph (e) of this section, school personnel may apply the relevant disciplinary procedures to children with disabilities in the same manner and for the same duration as the procedures would be applied to children without disabilities, except as provided in paragraph (d) of this section.

(d) Services.

(1) A child with a disability who is removed from the child's current placement pursuant to paragraphs (c), or (g) of this section must—

(i) Continue to receive educational services, as provided in § 300.101(a), so as to enable the child to continue to participate in the general education curriculum, although in another setting, and to progress toward meeting the goals set out in the child's IEP; and

(ii) Receive, as appropriate, a functional behavioral assessment, and behavioral intervention services and modifications, that are designed to address the behavior violation so that it does not recur.

(2) The services required by paragraph (d)(1), (d)(3), (d)(4), and (d)(5) of this section may be provided in an interim alternative educational setting.

(3) A public agency is only required to provide services during periods of removal to a child with a disability who has been removed from his or her current placement for 10 school days or less in that school year, if it provides services to a child without disabilities who is similarly removed.

(4) After a child with a disability has been removed from his or her current placement for 10 school days in the same school year, if the current removal is for not more than 10 consecutive school days and is not a change of placement under § 300.536, school personnel, in consultation with at least one of the child's teachers, determine the extent to which services are needed, as provided in § 300.101(a), so as to enable the child to continue to participate in the general education curriculum, although in another setting, and to progress toward meeting the goals set out in the child's IEP.

(5) If the removal is a change of placement under § 300.536, the child's IEP Team determines appropriate services under paragraph (d)(1) of this section.

(e) Manifestation determination.

(1) Within 10 school days of any decision to change the placement of a child with a disability because of a violation of a code of student conduct, the LEA, the parent, and relevant members of the child's IEP Team (as determined by the parent and the LEA) must review all relevant information in the student's file, including the child's IEP, any teacher observations, and any relevant information provided by the parents to determine—

(i) If the conduct in question was caused by, or had a direct and substantial relationship to, the child's disability; or

(ii) If the conduct in question was the direct result of the LEA's failure to implement the IEP.

(2) The conduct must be determined to be a manifestation of the child's disability if the LEA, the parent, and relevant members of the child's IEP Team determine that a condition in either paragraph (e)(1)(i) or (1)(ii) of this section was met.

(3) If the LEA, the parent, and relevant members of the child's IEP Team determine the condition described in paragraph (e)(1)(ii) of this section was met, the LEA must take immediate steps to remedy those deficiencies.

(f) Determination that behavior was a manifestation. If the LEA, the parent, and relevant members of the IEP Team make the determination that the conduct was a manifestation of the child's disability, the IEP Team must—

(1) Either—

(i) Conduct a functional behavioral assessment, unless the LEA had conducted a functional behavioral assessment before the behavior that resulted in the change of placement occurred, and implement a behavioral intervention plan for the child; or

(ii) If a behavioral intervention plan already has been developed, review the behavioral intervention plan, and modify it, as necessary, to address the behavior; and

(2) Except as provided in paragraph (g) of this section, return the child to the placement from which the child was removed, unless the parent and the LEA agree to a change of placement as part of the modification of the behavioral intervention plan.

(g) Special circumstances. School personnel may remove a student to an interim alternative educational setting for not more than 45 school days without regard to whether the behavior is determined to be a manifestation of the child's disability, if the child—

(1) Carries a weapon to or possesses a weapon at school, on school premises, or to or at a school function under the jurisdiction of an SEA or an LEA;

(2) Knowingly possesses or uses illegal drugs, or sells or solicits the sale of a controlled substance, while at school, on school premises, or at a school function under the jurisdiction of an SEA or an LEA; or

(3) Has inflicted serious bodily injury upon another person while at school, on school premises, or at a school function under the jurisdiction of an SEA or an LEA.

(h) Notification. On the date on which the decision is made to make a removal that constitutes a change of placement of a child with a disability because of a violation of a code of student conduct, the LEA must notify the parents of that decision, and provide the parents the procedural safeguards notice described in § 300.504.

(i) Definitions. For purposes of this section, the following definitions apply:

(1) Controlled substance means a drug or other substance identified under schedules I, II, III, IV, or V in section 202(c) of the Controlled Substances Act (21 U.S.C. 812(c)).

(2) Illegal drug means a controlled substance; but does not include a controlled substance that is legally possessed or used under the supervision of a licensed health-care professional or that is legally possessed or used under any other authority under that Act or under any other provision of Federal law.

(3) Serious bodily injury has the meaning given the term "serious bodily injury" under paragraph (3) of subsection (h) of section 1365 of title 18, United States Code.

(4) Weapon has the meaning given the term "dangerous weapon" under paragraph (2) of the first subsection (g) of section 930 of title 18, United States Code.

(Authority: 20 U.S.C. 1415(k)(1) and (7))

SOURCE: 71 FR 46755, Aug. 14, 2006; 72 FR 17781, April 9, 2007; 80 FR 23666, April 28, 2015, unless otherwise noted.

AUTHORITY: 20 U.S.C. 1221e–3, 1406, 1411–1419, 3474, unless otherwise noted

Notes of Decisions (13)

Current through March 24, 2016; 81 FR 16051.

| End of Document | © 2016 Thomson Reuters. No claim to original U.S. Government Works. |

Code of Federal Regulations
Title 34. Education
Subtitle B. Regulations of the Offices of the Department of Education
Chapter III. Office of Special Education and Rehabilitative Services, Department of Education
Part 300. Assistance to States for the Education of Children with Disabilities (Refs & Annos)
Subpart E. Procedural Safeguards
Discipline Procedures

34 C.F.R. § 300.531

§ 300.531 Determination of setting.

Effective: October 13, 2006

Currentness

The child's IEP Team determines the interim alternative educational setting for services under § 300.530(c), (d)(5), and (g).

(Authority: 20 U.S.C. 1415(k)(2))

SOURCE: 71 FR 46755, Aug. 14, 2006; 72 FR 17781, April 9, 2007; 80 FR 23666, April 28, 2015, unless otherwise noted.

AUTHORITY: 20 U.S.C. 1221e–3, 1406, 1411–1419, 3474, unless otherwise noted.

Notes of Decisions (1)

Current through March 24, 2016; 81 FR 16051.

| End of Document | © 2016 Thomson Reuters. No claim to original U.S. Government Works. |

Code of Federal Regulations
Title 34. Education
Subtitle B. Regulations of the Offices of the Department of Education
Chapter III. Office of Special Education and Rehabilitative Services, Department of Education
Part 300. Assistance to States for the Education of Children with Disabilities (Refs & Annos)
Subpart E. Procedural Safeguards
Discipline Procedures

34 C.F.R. § 300.532

§ 300.532 Appeal.

Effective: October 13, 2006

Currentness

(a) General. The parent of a child with a disability who disagrees with any decision regarding placement under §§ 300.530 and 300.531, or the manifestation determination under § 300.530(e), or an LEA that believes that maintaining the current placement of the child is substantially likely to result in injury to the child or others, may appeal the decision by requesting a hearing. The hearing is requested by filing a complaint pursuant to §§ 300.507 and 300.508(a) and (b).

(b) Authority of hearing officer.

(1) A hearing officer under § 300.511 hears, and makes a determination regarding an appeal under paragraph (a) of this section.

(2) In making the determination under paragraph (b)(1) of this section, the hearing officer may—

(i) Return the child with a disability to the placement from which the child was removed if the hearing officer determines that the removal was a violation of § 300.530 or that the child's behavior was a manifestation of the child's disability; or

(ii) Order a change of placement of the child with a disability to an appropriate interim alternative educational setting for not more than 45 school days if the hearing officer determines that maintaining the current placement of the child is substantially likely to result in injury to the child or to others.

(3) The procedures under paragraphs (a) and (b)(1) and (2) of this section may be repeated, if the LEA believes that returning the child to the original placement is substantially likely to result in injury to the child or to others.

(c) Expedited due process hearing.

(1) Whenever a hearing is requested under paragraph (a) of this section, the parents or the LEA involved in the dispute must have an opportunity for an impartial due process hearing consistent with the requirements of §§ 300.507 and

300.508(a) through (c) and §§ 300.510 through 300.514, except as provided in paragraph (c)(2) through (4) of this section.

(2) The SEA or LEA is responsible for arranging the expedited due process hearing, which must occur within 20 school days of the date the complaint requesting the hearing is filed. The hearing officer must make a determination within 10 school days after the hearing.

(3) Unless the parents and LEA agree in writing to waive the resolution meeting described in paragraph (c)(3)(i) of this section, or agree to use the mediation process described in § 300.506—

(i) A resolution meeting must occur within seven days of receiving notice of the due process complaint; and

(ii) The due process hearing may proceed unless the matter has been resolved to the satisfaction of both parties within 15 days of the receipt of the due process complaint.

(4) A State may establish different State-imposed procedural rules for expedited due process hearings conducted under this section than it has established for other due process hearings, but, except for the timelines as modified in paragraph (c)(3) of this section, the State must ensure that the requirements in §§ 300.510 through 300.514 are met.

(5) The decisions on expedited due process hearings are appealable consistent with § 300.514.

(Authority: 20 U.S.C. 1415(k)(3) and (4)(B), 1415(f)(1)(A))

SOURCE: 71 FR 46755, Aug. 14, 2006; 72 FR 17781, April 9, 2007; 80 FR 23666, April 28, 2015, unless otherwise noted.

AUTHORITY: 20 U.S.C. 1221e–3, 1406, 1411–1419, 3474, unless otherwise noted.

Current through March 24, 2016; 81 FR 16051.

| End of Document | © 2016 Thomson Reuters. No claim to original U.S. Government Works. |

Code of Federal Regulations
Title 34. Education
Subtitle B. Regulations of the Offices of the Department of Education
Chapter III. Office of Special Education and Rehabilitative Services, Department of Education
Part 300. Assistance to States for the Education of Children with Disabilities (Refs & Annos)
Subpart E. Procedural Safeguards
Discipline Procedures

34 C.F.R. § 300.533

§ 300.533 Placement during appeals.

Effective: October 30, 2007

Currentness

When an appeal under § 300.532 has been made by either the parent or the LEA, the child must remain in the interim alternative educational setting pending the decision of the hearing officer or until the expiration of the time period specified in § 300.530(c) or (g), whichever occurs first, unless the parent and the SEA or LEA agree otherwise.

(Authority: 20 U.S.C. 1415(k)(4)(A))

Credits

[72 FR 61307, Oct. 30, 2007]

SOURCE: 71 FR 46755, Aug. 14, 2006; 72 FR 17781, April 9, 2007; 80 FR 23666, April 28, 2015, unless otherwise noted.

AUTHORITY: 20 U.S.C. 1221e–3, 1406, 1411–1419, 3474, unless otherwise noted.

Notes of Decisions (2)

Current through March 24, 2016; 81 FR 16051.

| End of Document | © 2016 Thomson Reuters. No claim to original U.S. Government Works. |

Code of Federal Regulations
Title 34. Education
Subtitle B. Regulations of the Offices of the Department of Education
Chapter III. Office of Special Education and Rehabilitative Services, Department of Education
Part 300. Assistance to States for the Education of Children with Disabilities (Refs & Annos)
Subpart E. Procedural Safeguards
Discipline Procedures

34 C.F.R. § 300.534

§ 300.534 Protections for children not determined eligible for special education and related services.

Effective: October 13, 2006

Currentness

(a) General. A child who has not been determined to be eligible for special education and related services under this part and who has engaged in behavior that violated a code of student conduct, may assert any of the protections provided for in this part if the public agency had knowledge (as determined in accordance with paragraph (b) of this section) that the child was a child with a disability before the behavior that precipitated the disciplinary action occurred.

(b) Basis of knowledge. A public agency must be deemed to have knowledge that a child is a child with a disability if before the behavior that precipitated the disciplinary action occurred—

(1) The parent of the child expressed concern in writing to supervisory or administrative personnel of the appropriate educational agency, or a teacher of the child, that the child is in need of special education and related services;

(2) The parent of the child requested an evaluation of the child pursuant to §§ 300.300 through 300.311; or

(3) The teacher of the child, or other personnel of the LEA, expressed specific concerns about a pattern of behavior demonstrated by the child directly to the director of special education of the agency or to other supervisory personnel of the agency.

(c) Exception. A public agency would not be deemed to have knowledge under paragraph (b) of this section if—

(1) The parent of the child—

(i) Has not allowed an evaluation of the child pursuant to §§ 300.300 through 300.311; or

(ii) Has refused services under this part; or

(2) The child has been evaluated in accordance with §§ 300.300 through 300.311 and determined to not be a child with a

disability under this part.

(d) Conditions that apply if no basis of knowledge.

(1) If a public agency does not have knowledge that a child is a child with a disability (in accordance with paragraphs (b) and (c) of this section) prior to taking disciplinary measures against the child, the child may be subjected to the disciplinary measures applied to children without disabilities who engage in comparable behaviors consistent with paragraph (d)(2) of this section.

(2)(i) If a request is made for an evaluation of a child during the time period in which the child is subjected to disciplinary measures under § 300.530, the evaluation must be conducted in an expedited manner.

(ii) Until the evaluation is completed, the child remains in the educational placement determined by school authorities, which can include suspension or expulsion without educational services.

(iii) If the child is determined to be a child with a disability, taking into consideration information from the evaluation conducted by the agency and information provided by the parents, the agency must provide special education and related services in accordance with this part, including the requirements of §§ 300.530 through 300.536 and section 612(a)(1)(A) of the Act.

(Authority: 20 U.S.C. 1415(k)(5))

SOURCE: 71 FR 46755, Aug. 14, 2006; 72 FR 17781, April 9, 2007; 80 FR 23666, April 28, 2015, unless otherwise noted.

AUTHORITY: 20 U.S.C. 1221e–3, 1406, 1411–1419, 3474, unless otherwise noted.

Notes of Decisions (2)

Current through March 24, 2016; 81 FR 16051.

| End of Document | © 2016 Thomson Reuters. No claim to original U.S. Government Works. |

Code of Federal Regulations
Title 34. Education
Subtitle B. Regulations of the Offices of the Department of Education
Chapter III. Office of Special Education and Rehabilitative Services, Department of Education
Part 300. Assistance to States for the Education of Children with Disabilities (Refs & Annos)
Subpart E. Procedural Safeguards
Discipline Procedures

34 C.F.R. § 300.535

§ 300.535 Referral to and action by law enforcement and judicial authorities.

Effective: October 13, 2006

Currentness

(a) Rule of construction. Nothing in this part prohibits an agency from reporting a crime committed by a child with a disability to appropriate authorities or prevents State law enforcement and judicial authorities from exercising their responsibilities with regard to the application of Federal and State law to crimes committed by a child with a disability.

(b) Transmittal of records.

(1) An agency reporting a crime committed by a child with a disability must ensure that copies of the special education and disciplinary records of the child are transmitted for consideration by the appropriate authorities to whom the agency reports the crime.

(2) An agency reporting a crime under this section may transmit copies of the child's special education and disciplinary records only to the extent that the transmission is permitted by the Family Educational Rights and Privacy Act.

(Authority: 20 U.S.C. 1415(k)(6))

SOURCE: 71 FR 46755, Aug. 14, 2006; 72 FR 17781, April 9, 2007; 80 FR 23666, April 28, 2015, unless otherwise noted.

AUTHORITY: 20 U.S.C. 1221e–3, 1406, 1411–1419, 3474, unless otherwise noted.

Notes of Decisions (1)

Current through March 24, 2016; 81 FR 16051.

Code of Federal Regulations
  Title 34. Education
    Subtitle B. Regulations of the Offices of the Department of Education
      Chapter III. Office of Special Education and Rehabilitative Services, Department of Education
        Part 300. Assistance to States for the Education of Children with Disabilities (Refs & Annos)
          Subpart E. Procedural Safeguards
            Discipline Procedures

34 C.F.R. § 300.536

§ 300.536 Change of placement because of disciplinary removals.

Effective: October 13, 2006

Currentness

(a) For purposes of removals of a child with a disability from the child's current educational placement under §§ 300.530 through 300.535, a change of placement occurs if—

(1) The removal is for more than 10 consecutive school days; or

(2) The child has been subjected to a series of removals that constitute a pattern—

(i) Because the series of removals total more than 10 school days in a school year;

(ii) Because the child's behavior is substantially similar to the child's behavior in previous incidents that resulted in the series of removals; and

(iii) Because of such additional factors as the length of each removal, the total amount of time the child has been removed, and the proximity of the removals to one another.

(b)(1) The public agency determines on a case-by-case basis whether a pattern of removals constitutes a change of placement.

(2) This determination is subject to review through due process and judicial proceedings.

(Authority: 20 U.S.C. 1415(k))

SOURCE: 71 FR 46755, Aug. 14, 2006; 72 FR 17781, April 9, 2007; 80 FR 23666, April 28, 2015, unless otherwise noted.

AUTHORITY: 20 U.S.C. 1221e–3, 1406, 1411–1419, 3474, unless otherwise noted.

Notes of Decisions (16)

Current through March 24, 2016; 81 FR 16051.

| End of Document | © 2016 Thomson Reuters. No claim to original U.S. Government Works. |

Code of Federal Regulations
  Title 34. Education
    Subtitle B. Regulations of the Offices of the Department of Education
      Chapter III. Office of Special Education and Rehabilitative Services, Department of Education
        Part 300. Assistance to States for the Education of Children with Disabilities (Refs & Annos)
          Subpart E. Procedural Safeguards
            Discipline Procedures

34 C.F.R. § 300.537

§ 300.537 State enforcement mechanisms.

Effective: October 13, 2006

Currentness

Notwithstanding §§ 300.506(b)(7) and 300.510(d)(2), which provide for judicial enforcement of a written agreement reached as a result of mediation or a resolution meeting, there is nothing in this part that would prevent the SEA from using other mechanisms to seek enforcement of that agreement, provided that use of those mechanisms is not mandatory and does not delay or deny a party the right to seek enforcement of the written agreement in a State court of competent jurisdiction or in a district court of the United States.

(Authority: 20 U.S.C. 1415(e)(2)(F), 1415(f)(1)(B))

SOURCE: 71 FR 46755, Aug. 14, 2006; 72 FR 17781, April 9, 2007; 80 FR 23666, April 28, 2015, unless otherwise noted.

AUTHORITY: 20 U.S.C. 1221e–3, 1406, 1411–1419, 3474, unless otherwise noted.

Current through March 24, 2016; 81 FR 16051.

End of Document	© 2016 Thomson Reuters. No claim to original U.S. Government Works.

Appendix L
Letter to Parent re: Subpoenaed Records

[Date]

[Name]
[Address]

Re: Subpoena for Student Records

Dear [Name]:

The [NAME]Unified School District is in receipt of a Subpoena Duces Tecum submitted by [Name of attorney requesting records], [Title of attorney requesting records, i.e. Public Defender Prosecutor, or just Attorney if Private], for [Name of county] County in regards to a case against the defendant [Name of Defendant]. [Name of attorney requesting records] is requesting the [Provide description of records requested as described in the declaration] for [Name of student whose records are being requested]. The subpoena requests that the Custodian of Records for the district make all of the above identified records of your child available.

The law requires that [Name of attorney requesting records] inform you of your rights, as parent of [Name of student whose records are being requested], to object to the production of records. In case you have not been notified, I am enclosing a copy of the subpoena.

The subpoena has been reviewed and we believe it to be valid. Both the Education Code and the Family Educational Rights and Privacy Act permit a school district to disclose student educational records without parental consent upon receipt of a lawfully issued subpoena (34 C.F.R. §99.31(a)(9)(ii); Ed. Code § 49077). In accordance with section 49077 of the Education Code, we are providing you this advance notice that the District is in receipt of a validly issued subpoena for the production of your children's records.

You have a legal right to object to the production of the requested records and/or to take further legal action. You may want to consult with an attorney for legal advice. However, you must take action prior to the scheduled date of production, [Date/time of production from Subpoena].

This is to inform you that if the District does not receive either a notice from you that you have objected to the production of records or a notice that you have filed a motion to squash the subpoena or seek a protective order, the District will be required to disclose the subpoenaed records.

If you have any questions regarding this matter, please feel free to contact me at [Contact phone number].

Sincerely,

[Name of person signing letter]
[Title of person signing letter]

Enclosures

Appendix M
Civility Letter

[Name]
[Address]

[Date]

Dear:

It has been brought to the [Name of District] District's attention that you engaged in verbally abusive, disruptive, and uncivil behavior [provide description of the conduct]

At this time, in accordance with Education Codes 32210 and 32211(b) and California Penal Code 626.8, I am formally directing you to stay off of the [Name of School] campus for a period of seven days due to the incident that occurred in [Date of incident]. You may not enter the [Name of School] campus until [Date of re-entry]. After the seven days stay-away period has passed, and if you have lawful business on the campus, you must follow District and school protocol whenever coming onto the [Name of School] campus by maintaining civil behavior while on or around the campus at all times.

The District takes the safety and welfare of all staff and students very seriously. It is not acceptable under any circumstances for a parent or other adult to willfully disrupt the school environment. Education Code 32210 states that any person who willfully disturbs any public school is guilty of a misdemeanor and can be fined up to $500. Education Code 32211(b) states that a person who causes a disturbance at school may be directed to leave *by* the Principal or designee, in which case the person shall not return to the school for a period of (7) seven days from the initial request. California Penal Code 626.8 states that it is a misdemeanor for any person to interfere with the peaceful conduct of school related activities. These laws ensure a safe and orderly environment at all schools throughout the District. I will be notifying the [Name of Police Department] Police Department of your actions. You are expected to immediately adhere to the directives outlined in this letter.

Respectfully,

[Name of person signing letter]

Appendix N
Cease and Desist Letter

February 14, _____

Mr./Mrs./Ms.
Address

Dear Mr./Mrs./Ms.:

As principal of Name of School, I am writing this letter on behalf of the [Name] Unified School District with regard to recent disruptive behavior you have engaged in on the Name of School campus. As administrator of this school, it is my primary responsibility to ensure the safety and well being of each student and staff member. You were involved in the following incident(s):

    On Date, you ….

    On Date, you ….

As a result of these incidents, you have caused employees, students, and parents to fear for their safety.

Pursuant to Education Code 44811 any parent, guardian, or other person, whose conduct, in a place where a school employee is required to be in the course of his or her duties, materially disrupts class work or extracurricular activities or involves substantial disorder is guilty of a misdemeanor. The misdemeanor is punishable by a fine of Five Hundred dollars ($500) to One Thousand dollars ($1,000), by imprisonment in the county jail for up to one year, or both.

Please be advised that if you wish to speak to or visit anyone at Name of School, you must make an appointment in advance by telephone with the principal. I will escort you during your time on campus. It is our expectation that you will conduct yourself in a respectful manner at all times while visiting the Name of School campus. When you arrive on campus for your appointment you will need to check in at the school office in accordance with our visitation procedure.

Please be advised that should you fail to comply with these guidelines, the District, without further notice, will immediately take all appropriate legal action to protect its students, teachers and staff. This may result in the District obtaining a restraining order barring you from the campus entirely. The District would prefer not to have to take such a step.

Please contact the undersigned with any questions or concerns regarding the foregoing.

Sincerely,

Your Name

Made in the USA
San Bernardino, CA
23 August 2016